FERVENT

FERVENT

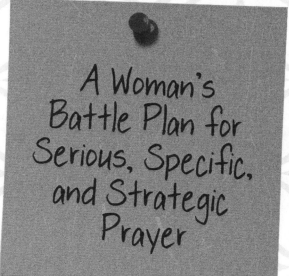

A Woman's Battle Plan for Serious, Specific, and Strategic Prayer

PRISCILLA SHIRER

B&H
PUBLISHING GROUP
NASHVILLE, TENNESSEE

For
Annie Eleen Cannings
Because you've taught me the power
of writing down my prayers

CONTENTS

Theoden: *I will not risk open war.*

Aragorn: *Open war is upon you, whether you would risk it or not.*

THE LORD OF THE RINGS: THE TWO TOWERS

THIS MEANS WAR

Just so you know what you're getting into . . .

By the time you've finished reading (and working) through this book, the front cover shouldn't be able to close neatly back over on itself. It should be noticeably disfigured. Ski-ramping up from the spine at such a scooped angle that even if you laid an old-school telephone book on top, you still couldn't smooth out what's become so harshly, permanently misshapen. From heartfelt use. War torn. An impossible option for regifting at Christmastime.

I'm expecting grass stains. Ink smears. Dog-ears. Battle scars. A few of those little wrinkly circles that form on the page when an accidental drop of tea, if not a tear escaping from your eye, spills across two or three lines of text. Unmistakable signs that you've been here and been involved here, invested here.

I want pages ripped out and written on. The edges tattered and the corners curled. I want your kids afraid to touch it without using plastic gloves. Perhaps even the salad tongs.

This book is just not meant for pretty reading. It's not for coffee-table curiosity and other such cameo appearances. Think of it instead as industrial-grade survival gear. Duct tape and superglue. Leather straps lashed around it. Old shoelaces maybe. In tight double knots. Whatever it takes to keep it all together.

Because this is war. The fight of your life. A very real enemy has been strategizing and scheming against you, assaulting you, coming after your emotions, your mind, your man, your child, your future. In fact, he's doing it right this second. Right where you're sitting. Right where you are.

But I say his reign of terror stops *here*. Stops *now*. He might keep coming, but he won't have victory anymore.

Because it all starts failing when we start praying.

Now if you want a book *about* prayer, this one's probably not for you. You can find some wonderful books on prayer by some scholarly writers, books that are well worth the time spent reading them. In fact, I highly suggest you do. Can't really learn too much about prayer, can you? But here, in these pages, we aren't going to merely *talk* about prayer or *think* about praying.

No.

Get ready.

To pray.

Because life is just too impossible otherwise—yours, mine, everybody's. We simply don't have the luxury of playing nice with prayer. Not if we want things to change. Not if we want to be free—from whatever's keeping us held down and held back. Not if we want our hearts whole and thriving and deep and grounded . . . different. Not if we want to reach our destinies and experience God's promises. Not if we want our husbands and children living out what God has called them to do and be and become. Not if we want a fence of God's protection around us. Not if we want to bear the unmistakable mark of His favor upon us. Not if we want the devil and his plans to go back to the hell where they came from.

But none of that is going to happen—no matter how badly we may want it—as long as prayer remains an afterthought, a formality, a mindless mix of duty and manipulation, something we do but usually don't do, and rarely if ever do with any meaning and vitality, with confidence and clarity. As a result, we waste a whole lot of years, doing a whole lot of other things. Things that thoroughly exhaust us but ultimately don't work. We end up, for all our trying, missing the point, missing out on what God intended, missing the whole heart of what really matters. So now we're going to pray specifically and strategically.

Praying with *precision* is key. When we pray about the places where we seriously suspect the enemy is at work—that's how we keep our prayers focused, not only on particular situations but on biblical truths that are consistent with maintaining victory in the midst of them. It's how our praying stays integrated with reality, rather than aimlessly wandering down a side, spiritual hallway that never seems to connect with the living room, where we, you know . . . live. It's how we keep our whole selves engaged and alert, trusting God for the right things, confident He's giving them, able to sense His direction about what to do and then to take action accordingly.

If all we're doing is flinging words and emotions in all directions without any real consideration for the specific ways the enemy is targeting us and the promises of God that apply to us, we're mostly just wasting our time. We're adding to the confusion while not really making a noticeable dent in the problem or the process. We're fighting to keep our heads above water, yet feeling pretty sure on most days we're fighting a losing battle.

Well, part of that idea is right: *WE ARE in a battle*. A battle with a long history that reaches back before the annals of time began. But it's one in which the victor has already been determined. A battle, yes. But a *losing battle?*

Not. Even. Possible.

And prayer is our not-so-secret weapon in the fight. I'd even venture to say, our most potent one.

I'm willing to admit, right up front, there's an undeniable, unknowable, invisible mystery to prayer. That's why our first reaction to it often leans toward dismissing it, downplaying it, devaluing its critical importance. Prayer, we think, is a good idea in theory, if only it actually did anything or made a difference. But here's the deal. Despite what we may or may not understand about prayer, God has deliberately chosen this particular vehicle as the one that drives His activity in people's lives. It's what He allows us to use to cooperate and partner with Him in the fulfilling of His will. He's created prayer as a primary way of putting us into personal contact with Him and with His eternal realities, any hour of the day or night.

So as we begin to grasp its significance, and as we practice implementing this incredible power tool He's placed in our hands, He divinely positions us—even a little life like ours—in His grand purposes for the ages. Through the connective tissue of prayer, He cracks open the door that makes us at least a small part of how these massive plans of His are translated into the lives of people we know.

Including ours.

Prayer is the portal that brings the power of heaven down to earth. It is kryptonite to the enemy and to all his ploys against you.

That's why you and I need this book. That's why this intersection of our life journeys in these pages is so crucial—not because of what I'm writing but because of what we are going to be doing with our time together—and what our God is going to be doing as a result.

You and I, once we've gotten just a little better acquainted, will begin actively crafting some prayer strategies tailor-made for your victory. We're going to do it by touching on the areas of your life that the enemy is targeting the hardest—the bulk of what frustrates you, worries you, defeats you, exasperates you, angers you, taunts you, deflates you, and sometimes makes impossible demands on you. And if you come to a chapter that doesn't seem to strike a red-hot chord with you now, read it anyway, because sooner or later it will. And then, at the end of each chapter, you'll compose a strategy of prayer in regard to your own life in that particular area. Then with your personalized prayer strategies in place—yanked right out of this book (did you notice the perforated pages in the back?)—then posted where you can regularly see them and read them and launch them against the enemy's most well-disguised hideouts—you'll be able to fight back as hard (and harder) than the one who's fighting against you.

Strategies? Yes. Because as you may have noticed, the battles your enemy wages against you—especially the most acute, consistent ones—possess a personality to them, an intimate knowledge of who you are and the precise pressure points where you can most easily be taken down. Random accident? Lucky guess? I don't think so. These areas of greatest fear and anxiety in your life are clues to some important spiritual information. They reveal, among other things, that a personalized strategy has been insidiously put in place to destroy your vibrancy and render you defeated. It's been drawn up on the blackboard by someone who knows where you live and whom you love, knows your customary tendencies, and knows from long experience how best to exploit every single one of them. And maybe up until now, it's been working.

But I assume, by your presence here, that you're sick of that. I know *I* most certainly am. Sick of losing these daily battles of mine. Sick of watching things deteriorate around me, as well as in the lives of those I care about. But what I'm beginning to understand is that I can't just go barreling into this fight blindly. I can't just throw something up against the wall and hope it sticks. I need a plan. Just as *you* need a plan. A strategy for war.

And funneled through the experiences outlined in this book, as well as through the specific work of God's Spirit in your life and (most importantly) the living power of God's Word, a number of personal prayer strategies will begin to develop. You're going to march out of here with some battle options that will not only help you deflect every assault trained against you but will allow you to actively advance against them—against scrappy, tenacious opposition. You'll be able to tread across stretches of high-voltage ground that you've never known how to navigate before, places that have always seemed too impossible to figure out. Through prayer you'll not only be able to defend yourself from incoming sniper fire but through Almighty God will be able to push into enemy territory and take . . . stuff . . . back.

Trust me, it can happen.

It *will* happen.

But not by happenstance. God's plan for you is to move you into a position of impact by infusing you with truth and employing you in prayer. You don't need to be a genius to do it. You don't need to learn ten-dollar words and be able to spout them with theological ease. You just need to bring your honest, transparent, available—and, let's just say it— your fed-up, over-it, stepped-on-your-last-nerve self, and be ready to become fervently relentless. All in His name.

At the end of the day, the enemy is going to be sorry he ever messed with you. You're about to become his worst nightmare a million times over. He thought he could wear you down, sure that after a while you'd give up without much of a fight.

Well, just wait till he encounters the fight of God's Spirit in you.

Because . . .

This.

Means.

War.

OPENING IN PRAYER

 To anybody else this photo probably wouldn't mean anything. No one would pay a lot of money or give large amounts of their attention to it. It wouldn't be to them the personal treasure it is to me. Because to them, it'd be just a photo. A random image.

Of two hands.

One of the hands, as you see, is wrinkled and worn. Visibly older. A couple of the nails are a bit bruised and tattered. There's no jewelry to adorn any finger. And no real attempt at cosmetic touches. It's just plain. Simple. Strong and storied, yet nobly, humbly feminine.

The second hand in the picture, lying just overtop the fingers of the first, is much younger and smoother. Brown— same color as the other, though with a skin texture that's still evenly composed and supple. Nails fairly neat and a tad more youthful. A ring on the fourth finger. Together, they're a quick portrait in chronological contrast.

But what I really love about this picture is what's lying beneath these two hands. That old spiral notebook. Grocery-store quality. A dollar forty-nine, plus tax, on sale. No expensive leather binding or intricately designed, acid-free paper. Just a fourth-grade composition book with wide-ruled, lined sheets and a plastic-coated cover.

And yet within those pages, bound by thin, metal rings slightly mashed out of shape by the pressure of frequent use, are the vast treasures of a living legacy.

These two hands—older and younger—belong to a grandmother and her granddaughter. And this spiral-bound filing cabinet contains a grandmother's prayer requests—written out, printed off, and prayed over, during her daily appointment with Jesus. She meets with Him the way she'd meet with any important friend—faithfully, personally, punctually. And in those early morning moments, she opens up this book of prayer and vocalizes her needs to Him, as well as the needs of others—requests she's been quietly gathering amid her daily dealings.

These two women, though separated by several decades of life experiences, go out together occasionally on little afternoon dates. And since a ninety-five-year-old metabolism can afford to indulge a predilection for McDonald's French fries and vanilla milk shakes, that's their usual outing. They drive through for a batch of that salty-sweet, hot-and-cold combination, then they meander random neighborhood streets, windows down, while the lip-smacking passenger munches to her heart's delight. But it's also in these moments, between her grandmother's swallows, when this grown grandchild seeks to absorb the treasured wisdom from nearly a century of holy living.

Recently on one of these fast-food sprees, when the subject of prayer came up, the younger asked the older why she wrote down her prayers in a notebook like that. Then she waited, even pushing the "record" button on her iPhone, hoping not to miss a word of what she knew would be a long, deeply spiritual answer—one she'd never want to forget and could pass down in her grandmother's own voice for generations to come.

They glanced at each other. No one spoke for a few moments. Another french fry. Long gulp of milk shake. Then came these understated words:

"So I won't forget."

Hmmh. And there you have it. The message of this whole book in one simple phrase. Straight from the tender lips of a godly grandma. You write out your prayers so you "won't forget" . . .

- won't forget who the real enemy is
- won't forget the One in whom your hope lies
- won't forget what your real need and dependencies are

- and later, won't forget the record of how God responds

Through intentional, deliberate, strategic prayer, you grab hold of Jesus and of everything He's already done on your behalf. It's how you tap into the power of heaven and watch it reverberate in your experiences. It's a key part of your offensive weaponry against a cunning foe who prowls around and watches for your weaknesses, your vulnerable places, for any opportunity to destroy you. In prayer you gain your strength—the power to gird yourself with armor that extinguishes every weapon your enemy wields.

Paul the apostle famously said it like this:

Put on all of God's armor so that you will be able to stand firm against all strategies of the devil. (Eph. 6:11 NLT)

There's that word again. *Strategies.* Schemes and deceptive plots being concocted for your demise by a very real enemy who is always primed to make his next move. He works overtime to destroy the relationships and circumstances you want to preserve. He laughs at your attempts to fix your own issues with timely words and hard work—tactics that might affect matters for a moment but can't begin to touch his underhanded, cunning efforts down where the root issues lie, or up in those spiritual "heavenly places" where such physical weapons were never meant to work. "For we are not fighting against flesh-and-blood enemies—"

- "but against evil rulers and authorities of the unseen world,"
- "against mighty powers in this dark world,"
- "and against evil spirits in the heavenly places." (v. 12 NLT)

So we strap on weapons that work—weapons divinely authorized for our success in spiritual warfare: the belt of truth, the breastplate of righteousness, the shoes of peace. Then we take up the shield of faith, the helmet of salvation, as well as the sword—the very Word of God. But we don't stop there. Because neither does Paul in his description of our spiritual armor in Ephesians 6—

Pray in the Spirit at all times and on every occasion. Stay alert and be persistent in your prayers for all believers everywhere. And pray . . . (vv. 18–19 NLT)

There it is. The fuel that drives everything. *Prayer.* We pray till our hands are worn and wrinkled. We pray until our granddaughters are old enough to understand and learn and copy our example. We pray until they can one day place their hands across ours, gently rubbing our aging skin, and we smile because now they'll never forget the things we had the good sense to record in writing for their generation. They will look back on our legacies and know we stood strong, fought the good fight, and finished a race in which we would *not even think* about letting the enemy have his way in our lives or in the lives of those we love.

We pray because our own solutions don't work and because prayer deploys, activates, and fortifies us against the attacks of the enemy. We pray because we're serious about taking back the ground he has sought to take from us.

That's what we do. And I hope it's what *you* do—or what you've come here to be renewed in doing. But make no mistake, this enemy will seek to discourage you from doing it. Dissuade you. Disarm you by putting a distaste for prayer in your mouth. He wants to see you passionless, powerless, and prayerless. Quiet. And because prayer is the divinely ordained mechanism that leads you into the heart and the power and the victory of Christ, he knows you'll remain defeated and undone without it. Tired and overwhelmed. Inching forward but mostly backward. Trying to figure out why the hope and enthusiasm you feel in church doesn't follow you to the four walls you live within.

And if I were your enemy, that's exactly what I'd want. I'd want to make you devalue the most potent weapons in your arsenal. I'd strategize against you, using carefully calculated methods to disorient and defeat you.

In fact, this approach makes so much devilish sense that it's exactly what the devil *does* do—to *you*, in *real life*—all under the umbrella of deception. He comes at you to . . . well, don't just listen to me; hear it from the loud voices who responded when I polled a large cross section of women, asking them to tell me the primary ways the enemy attacks them. After boiling down all their answers into the most common categories of responses, I ended up with what I believe to be a top ten of his favorite strategies. Here's where he seems to direct them against you the hardest:

Strategy 1—Against Your Passion

He seeks to dim your whole desire for prayer, dull your interest in spiritual things, and downplay the potency of your most strategic weapons (Eph. 6:10–20).

Strategy 2—Against Your Focus

He disguises himself and manipulates your perspective so you end up focusing on the wrong culprit, directing your weapons at the wrong enemy (2 Cor. 11:14).

Strategy 3—Against Your Identity

He magnifies your insecurities, leading you to doubt what God says about you and to disregard what He's given you (Eph. 1:17–19).

Strategy 4—Against Your Family

He wants to disintegrate your family, dividing your home, rendering it chaotic, restless, and unfruitful (Gen. 3:1–7).

Strategy 5—Against Your Confidence

He constantly reminds you of your past mistakes and bad choices, hoping to convince you that you're under God's judgment rather than under the blood (Rev. 12:10).

Strategy 6—Against Your Calling

He amplifies fear, worry, and anxiety until they're the loudest voices in your head, causing you to deem the adventure of following God too risky to attempt (Josh. 14:8).

Strategy 7—Against Your Purity

He tries to tempt you toward certain sins, convincing you that you can tolerate them without risking consequence, knowing they'll only wedge distance between you and God (Isa. 59:1–2).

Strategy 8—Against Your Rest and Contentment

He hopes to overload your life and schedule, pressuring you to constantly push beyond your limits, never feeling permission to say no (Deut. 5:15).

Strategy 9—Against Your Heart

He uses every opportunity to keep old wounds fresh in mind, knowing that anger and hurt and bitterness and unforgiveness will continue to roll the damage forward (Heb. 12:15).

Strategy 10—Against Your Relationships

He creates disruption and disunity within your circle of friends and within the shared community of the body of Christ (1 Tim. 2:8).

And that's just ten of 'em—ten of the most usual ways he strategizes against the strength of God's woman.

Well, two can play at that game. And with God on our side taking the lead in setting our own strategy plans, we're already in the vast majority. But we must still be diligent and intentional. We must recognize and cry out against the highly personalized attacks being thrown in our direction. No, there's no need to fear, but we'd better be on our guard. And we'd better not ever forget—like the grandmother in the picture says—to keep praying with purpose and precision, the way she prays for people like her granddaughter.

A granddaughter who just happens to be . . .

Me.

My name is written in that book of hers. Has been for decades. She's prayed for me since before I was born, asking God to gird and strengthen, to guide and sustain.

That was back when she, like me, once wore a wedding ring on one of those precious fingers, before her husband of more than fifty years, my grandfather, went ahead of her into heaven. But it occurs to me, as I look back at this photograph, that the wedding ring on *my* hand—and the strong, happy, trial-tested marriage it represents—is not attributable to my own abilities and fine behavior as much as it's a direct result of my name being in her book and of her firm resolve to fight for me. For my husband. For our family.

My grandmother, Annie Eleen Cannings—the woman to whom I've dedicated this book—has gone to war for me. On her knees. In prayer.

Fervent prayer.

And I've decided I want to follow her there.

So with my grandmother's keen instructions in tow, and with the truth of God's Word as my anchor on ultimate truth and reality, I've started the well-worn, proven discipline of writing down my prayers. I began by considering my most pressing dilemmas—the ones raging in my own heart, my family, my finances, my health, my ministry—and then started writing down my own battle plans for dealing with them, based on the truths of Scripture. I resolved to stop using physical means to fight battles that require spiritual remedies, using instead the power of prayer to do what it's always been designed to do.

I'm certainly not perfect at it, but I'm trying to grow.

They're posted in my closet now. My prayers, I mean. Seriously. Some are on full sheets of lined paper. Others are on little slivers of computer paper, ripped away after only a sentence or two. Or even just a word or two. But big or small, I've dated them and posted them all. And now, there they sit, taped right above a row of hooks in the closet where I see them every time I get dressed.

That way, *I won't forget.*

Those strategies help me remember to pray. And *what* to pray. And in doing so, I get dressed up in my spiritual armor, even while I'm getting dressed for the day.

That's what this book is all about. From my grandmother's heart to yours. Leading you to deliberately and thoughtfully write down your prayer strategies—tearing them right out of this book if you like—then posting them in a strategic place where you can pray them regularly and consistently.

INTO PRAYER

Couple of things to mention here, though, before we start to develop some intentional strategies of devil-busting prayer, designed to counteract his specific strategies against us. Whenever the conversation of demonic activity comes up in a book like this, most people scatter to one of two extremes. Either they *overestimate* Satan's influence and power, living with an inflated, erroneous perspective of his abilities. Or they *underestimate* him. They don't assign him any credit at all for the difficulties he's stirring up beneath the surface of their lives. One extreme leaves you saddled with undue fear and anxiety; the other just makes you stupid—(*too blunt to say it like that? sorry*)—unaware and completely open to every single attack.

Which of these categories do you fall into or lean toward? Either?

Let's be clear, no matter which way you gravitate, *Satan is not God*. And he is not God's counterpart or peer. They're not even on the same playing field. His influence, authority, and power don't even touch the fringe of what our Lord is capable of doing. Read ahead to Revelation 19 and 20 sometime, the so-called titanic clash of end-time foes in what's commonly known as the battle of Armageddon. Know what it really is? More like the devil and his demons getting all dressed up with no place to go. It's over before it even starts. The only thing that makes it a war is that he becomes a *prisoner* of war. Satan is nothing but a copycat, trying desperately to convince you he's more powerful than he actually is. Because remember: he does have limitations—boundaries he cannot cross no matter how much he desires or how hard he tries. For instance . . .

- He can't be everywhere at once (only God is omnipresent).

- He can't read your mind (only God is omniscient).

- He is merely an illusionist, using cunning trickery to deceive and mislead (only God can work flat-out, unmistakable miracles).

And last, but certainly not least . . .

- He's running out of time (our God is eternal).

So even though he's been given temporary clearance to strategize and antagonize, we don't need to pray from a position of fear or weakness against him. Quite the opposite. You and I, coming to the Father through the mighty name of Jesus, can pray like the victorious saints of God we've been empowered to be. And we can expect to prevail. *But* we can't expect to experience this power unless we're serious about joining the battle in prayer.

All right, then—before we get going—here are just a few bits and pieces of framework that might help you in getting started. We'll be using these reminders throughout to help the prayers you write stay anchored and strong:

- **P**—*Praise:* Thanksgiving is one of the most important aspects of prayer. It's not just a means of warming up (or buttering up). It's not just a preamble before getting down to what we really came to say. Gratitude to God for who He is and what He's already done should thread throughout every prayer because ultimately His name and His fame are the only reasons any of this matters.

- **R**—*Repentance:* God's real desire, in addition to displaying His glory, is to claim your heart and the hearts of those you love. So prayer, while it's certainly a place to deal with the objectives and details we want to see happening in our circumstances, is also about what's happening on the inside, where real transformation occurs. Expect prayer to expose where you're still resisting Him—not only resisting His *commands* but resisting the manifold blessings and benefits He gives to those who follow. Line your strategies with repentance: the courage to trust, and turn, and walk His way.

- **A**—*Asking:* Make your requests known. Be personal and specific. Write down details of your own issues and difficulties as they relate to the broader issue we discussed in that chapter, as well as how you perhaps see the enemy's hand at work in them or where you suspect he might be aiming next. You're not begging; you've been invited to ask, seek, and knock. God's expecting you. He's wanting you here. The best place to look is to Him.

- **Y**—*Yes:* "All of God's promises," the Bible says, "have been fulfilled in Christ with a resounding 'Yes!'" (2 Cor. 1:20 NLT). You may not understand what all's happening in your life right now, but any possible explanation pales in comparison to what you *do* know because of your faith in God's goodness and assurances. So allow your prayer to be accentuated with His own words from Scripture, His promises to you that correspond to your need. (I'll provide lots of options in each chapter to choose from.) There is nothing more powerful than praying God's own Word.

Praying like this, you can expect God to respond in accordance with His own sovereign, eternal will and His boundless love for you. Or as someone more clever than I has said . . .

> **P**rayer
> **R**eleases
> **A**ll
> **Y**our
> **E**ternal
> **R**esources

I like that.

But if you're still uneasy about it all, if you're not sure you'll know how to get the hang of this . . . no worries. With the next page you turn, you're entering the prayer strategy zone. And I guarantee you, God's Spirit is going to show you exactly how to get started.

Speaking of which . . . why don't we do just that: get
started.

If you've had it, then let's do it.

Let's get after it.

Let's pray.

Acrostic used on previous page: Richard A. Burr, *Developing Your Secret Closet of Prayer* (Camp Hill, PA: Christian Publications, 2008), 44.

YOUR PASSION

GETTING IT BACK WHEN IT'S GONE

If I were your enemy, I'd seek to dim your passion, dull your interest in spiritual things, dampen your belief in God's ability and His personal concern for you, and convince you that the hope you've lost is never coming back—and was probably just a lie to begin with.

Fervent prayer is fueled by passion.

By faith. By fire.

When everything else inside you is pulling you in twenty million different directions—off to the next busy thing in your busy day, if not off to bed and off the clock—passion is what plasters your knees to that floor. And digs in for dear life. It's your oomph. Your hutzpah. Your cutting edge.

Passion is what pushes the athlete to run one more lap, to crunch through one more set of reps. It's what silences those screaming thigh and stomach muscles, making them do what their owner demands of them, no matter how loudly they complain. *Passion* is what keeps a piano player anchored to the practice bench when no one else is around to notice the effort or give a pat on the back for approval. *Passion* is what inspires the eager young employee to outperform expectations, instead of just punching the clock to earn a paycheck like everybody else. *Passion* is what burns up the road between a child in danger and a parent in pursuit. It glows red-hot. And goes on driving. And grows even larger, the larger the obstacles become.

Passion is the fuel in the engine of your purpose. It's your "want-to." It's what keeps you going when mundane tasks bore you or difficult ones dissuade you. Passion is what keeps you moving in the direction your best intentions want you to go.

That's why, if I were your enemy, I'd make stealing your *passion* one of my primary goals. Because I know if I could dim your passion, I could significantly lower your resistance to temptation and discouragement. I could make you walk with a spiritual limp and lengthen how long it takes you to recover from the injury. If I could chip away at your zeal, at your hope, at your belief in God and what He can do, I could chisel down your faith to a whimper. Make you want to quit. And never try again. I'd cup an ear in your direction, hear nothing in your voice that sounds like anything but token prayer, and snicker at my success. Chalk another one up to my "Passion Elimination Plan"—the one with your name on it.

That's what I'd do. If I were your enemy.

I'd weaken your passion, your cutting edge—knowing full well that weak, impotent prayers (or better yet, prayerlessness) would follow right behind.

So take a long, hard, deep look at yourself and answer this question: Have you lost your passion? Has your get-up-and-go simply gotten-up-and-gone?

Maybe you've prayed and prayed for the same thing, over and over. . . . Maybe you've wanted God's will so bad, and wanted life to look different for so long. . . . Maybe you're feeling utterly discouraged or disappointed right now and not sure why you keep being surprised every time the same ol' thing keeps happening again and again. . . . Maybe other demands and distractions have leaked into your heart over time, crowding out space where older, nobler priorities once ruled. I get all of that. I've felt a lot of that.

But what makes you think it's somehow all *God's* fault? Or *your* fault? Or *everybody else's* fault? But never the *enemy's* fault? Why aren't we equally as quick to recognize the telltale marks of *his* darkened ideas and initiative?

When you can't seem to respond to spiritual stimuli with the same optimism and obedience as you once did, why do you think it could only be attributable to your bad character? To a drop in your hormone levels? To the normal deterioration that comes from age and accumulated adversity?

Maybe another less noticeable but equally probable reason is that you've been a victim of satanic sabotage. It's a *strategy*. Against *you*. On *purpose*. An assault launched with pinpoint planning and detail.

I mean, think about it. Doesn't it fit the profile?

Satan is a full-time *accuser*. He does it "day and night," the Bible says (Rev. 12:10). Instead of *convicting* you for the purpose of restoration, as God's Spirit does, he *condemns* you for the purpose of destroying, humiliating.

This pattern, by the way, is classic proof of the enemy's influence. Watch for it, and note his fingerprints. *Condemnation* always leads to guilt-laden discouragement, while *conviction*—though often painful in pointing out our wrongdoing—still somehow encourages and lifts us, giving us hope to rebuild on. The first makes you focus on yourself; the other points you to the grace and empowering mercy of Christ. To hear the devil tell it, these weaknesses of yours are reason for nothing but wretched despair; yet God says those same weaknesses are reason for your purest worship and gratitude. Your need for God's grace is supposed to be a passion enhancer. That's the *opposite* of what takes place, however, as soon as you start believing the enemy's accusations. He'll make you think God doesn't hear your prayers or respond to them—why?—because of *you*.

How typical. Because Satan, in addition to being an accuser, is also a confirmed *liar*. No . . . worse. He's the "father of lies" (John 8:44). The granddaddy of all untruth. Deception is the overarching umbrella that encompasses all His plans and programs.

He warps your perspective on the current events in your life until reality appears much worse and more desperate than it truly is. I'm not saying your situation is not legitimately bad; perhaps it is painful beyond description. But through his lying eyes, any passion for perseverance seems like a silly, sentimental waste of time. And yet he has the gall to insinuate that *God* is the one who lies to you, that any delay in the Lord's visible response to your prayer is open-and-shut evidence that He doesn't really hear you like He says. Or if He does, He apparently doesn't mind seeing you writhe in discomfort while you wait on His own sweet timing.

Such biting accusations against you, against God.

Such bitter lies about what's really taking place.

Those are just some of the ways he tries to eat away at your passion. Not overtly and conspicuously. He's much too crafty for that. But cunningly. Slowly. Incrementally. Over time.

And sometimes he gets us. We don't recognize it's him at first, working behind the scenes. We think the reason we've stopped praying is because—oh, "we just don't feel like it anymore." And sure—maybe, *maybe,* that's the way it really is. But possibly, *possibly,* this lack of feeling is a clue that the enemy's strategy has begun to take effect. He's worked you down enough until you can't seem to muster up the will to fight back, to keep believing for and praying about . . .

Your marriage . . . still hopelessly tense and broken.

Your child . . . still rebelling against all sound logic.

Your money . . . still not enough to feel like enough.

Your health . . . still as chronic or scary as ever.

Your addictions . . . still defeating you way too often.

You just can't seem to bring these up to God anymore because there doesn't seem to be any spiritual fire burning inside. Maybe even right now—even while reading a book that's inviting you back where you once walked, back to fervent, believing prayer—you honestly just don't see the point in going there again.

So here's what I'd say to you. *Let's start here.* Praying for this. To recover and maintain your passion. To regain and sustain your cutting edge.

In order to do it, I want to take you back to a real-life story that God placed in Scripture (2 Kings 6:1–7) for just such a moment as this. And I want to use it and the principles it teaches to encourage your heart and then help you begin stirring up a strategy to *get your passion back.* Because if you're not at a low-passion point right now, the time will likely come when you'll feel yourself being tugged there. And when that season comes, make a note to put this story on your must-read list.

As it happened, the prophet Elisha was standing near one of his protégés, who was chopping down a tree at the banks of the Jordan River, laboring to gather the raw materials needed for building a larger meeting place. But at one point in either an upswing or a downswing, the iron head of that man's ax wiggled loose from its wooden handle and sailed into the water, plopping to the bottom.

[Splash.] [Gasp.]

And just like that, he'd lost his cutting edge.

The young prophet was horrified. Not only had he lost the one tool on hand—the most important tool in the toolbox for moving him toward the outcome he desired—but the ax he'd been using had been borrowed from a friend. The ker-plunk of that dead weight in the water was a double whammy of disappointment and disgust. He couldn't go forward with his building project, and now he'd need to go to the person who'd loaned him the ax and tell what happened to it, that he'd broken it, lost it, that there was no getting it back.

Notice, though, these encouraging details from the story:

Number 1: *Despite the lost ax head, the presence of God was still near.* In ancient Israel, Yahweh's prophets were representations of His presence and power with His people. So when the man in this story lost the ax head, the fact that the prophet Elisha was right there alongside him (v. 3) wasn't just a simple comfort. It mattered that Elisha had seen how hard this man had worked, all the trees he'd chopped down, and how his cutting edge had been lost. It mattered that God's presence and the man's loss occurred within close proximity to the other. Satan would like to convince you that your lack of passion is an indication that God was either never there at all or has gotten disgusted with you and left. He wants you to believe that God has not seen your struggle and is unaware or disinterested in the details of your life. But just because you're feeling at a loss for words and "want-to"—just because your "cutting edge" in prayer seems misplaced for now—does not mean that God isn't close by.

Number 2: *The servant was doing something good when he lost his cutting edge.* He was being productive, building a new dwelling for himself and for those others involved in the school of the prophets (v. 2). In fact, if he hadn't been working so hard—if he'd just been sitting around doing nothing—there's little chance the ax would've ever become gradually loosened and ultimately dislodged. This tells me that being engaged in good, even godly, productive things is not an automatic guard against losing your cutting edge. In fact, one of Satan's dirtiest little tactics is to sneak in and steal it while you're square in the middle of investing yourself in worthwhile activities. That's why when you're sensing a drag in your faith, in your spiritual fire, it can sometimes simply mean you're doing exactly what you're supposed to be doing . . . and doing it well, at that.

Number 3: *The ax was borrowed* (v. 5). The presence of passion, faith, and belief in our hearts is a gift. It's on loan to our souls. Like the man's ax, our passion and spiritual fervor come from Someone else as a gift to us. If you've ever cried out passionately to God in faith, fully believing that He is able to do more than you ask or think or imagine, it's only because He first stirred up that passion within you. So instead of always feeling guilty—personally responsible—whenever your passion in prayer is weak or missing, realize instead that it is God's work both to give it and then to fan it into flame inside you. Which means you cannot manufacture it on your own. Your enemy, however—coy as he is—wants to burden you with blame for not having something that didn't originate with you in the first place. Don't fall for that.

Number 4: *Only a work of God could retrieve the ax head*. "'Where did it fall?' the man of God asked. When he showed him the place, Elisha cut a stick and threw it into the water at that spot. Then the ax head floated to the surface" (v. 6 NLT). Miraculously, by Elisha's hand, the slab of iron rustled free from the murky riverbed and bobbed up to the surface as if it were nothing but a floating chunk of driftwood. There it was! His cutting edge was back! Divinely recovered. Elisha's servant had understandably been convinced there was no hope of ever seeing it again.

And there *wouldn't* have been . . . except that he went to
Elisha. God, through the prophet, stepped in and made it
reappear. If the ax head had just dropped onto the ground,
anybody who saw where it went—including the man himself—could've picked it up and salvaged it. Instead it was
deep in the river. Only a miracle could get it back.

Just like *you* might need a miracle to get *yours* back, too,
if it's sunk to the bottom—like everyone's passion for prayer
has done at one time or another.

Listen to me. Nothing—*nothing!*—is too far gone that
your God cannot resurrect it. Even your cutting edge. So go
to Him to get it back. Don't try to regain it yourself. Don't
set your hopes on other people or circumstances to fuse it
back into the fiber of your being. Trust it into God's care.
Only His miraculous work can make it bubble back up to
the surface where it belongs. And He is more than willing
to do it.

CALL TO PRAYER

So here we go. Before we tackle and craft prayer strategies for the nine other topics in this book, the seminal matter of getting and maintaining our cutting edge so that we
even *want* to pray again is foundational.

But when we talk about *passion* in prayer, I sure don't
want to leave the impression that the only prayer God hears
is the kind that's spoken at high volume, with sweat and

tears and shaking fists and extraordinary energy. Prayer can be *silent* and still seethe with passion. And on some days, at some times, prayer—for any of us—can start out as simply an obedient appointment, an act of discipline, showing up in that prayer closet because it's the appointed time that we said we'd be there.

Because praying—reaching outward and upward to Him—is the way His passion comes down. Even prayers that begin with the blunt edge of willpower, dragging your heart along kicking and screaming, can soon begin to shine with the *cutting edge* of hope, faith, and passionate confidence in Christ. Once the wind of God's Spirit starts blowing, you're no longer praying rote, innocuous prayers. Instead, you're praying deliberate prayers. Prayers that are as personalized and devastating as the enemy's attacks against you. Strategic prayers. Powerful prayers. Prayers that tell the enemy his cover has been blown, his number has come up, and his game is done. Prayers built on the promises of God that entreat Him to give you back what He was responsible for giving you in the first place.

Infuse your first prayer strategy with passages and promises like these:

Create in me a clean heart, O God,
and renew a steadfast spirit within me. (Ps. 51:10)

∽

The LORD's lovingkindnesses indeed never cease,
   for His compassions never fail.
They are new every morning;
great is Your faithfulness. (Lam. 3:22–23)

∾

I will give them a heart to know Me, for I am the
LORD; and they will be My people, and I will be
their God, for they will return to Me with their
whole heart. (Jer. 24:7)

∾

Call upon Me and come and pray to Me, and I
will listen to you. You will seek Me and find Me
when you search for Me with all your heart. (Jer.
29:12–13)

∾

The LORD your God will circumcise your heart and
the heart of your descendants, to love the LORD your
God with all your heart and with all your soul, so
that you may live. (Deut. 30:6)

∾

Love the Lord your God with all your heart, and
with all your soul, and with all your mind, and with
all your strength. (Mark 12:30)

⤸

For where your treasure is, there your heart will be
also. (Luke 12:34)

⤸

I will give you a new heart and put a new spirit
within you; I will remove your heart of stone and
give you a heart of flesh. (Ezek. 36:26 HCSB)

Don't read that last one too quickly, OK? One more
time. Slowly. Deliberately. Like how you'd sip a glass of
sweet tea on a blazing hot summer day, wanting the refreshment to last.

Do you see the promise? "I will *give* you." "I will *remove*
your heart of stone" and "*give* you" a heart that's alive and
tender again, one that's beating and responsive again.
Engaged again. Able to believe again.

A prayer that's seeking passion should not be about
manufacturing a better feeling or jostling up a better mood.
It's simply about holding out your open hands—in thanksgiving first, in gratitude for God's faithfulness and His goodness and His assured, accomplished victory over the enemy.
Then asking. Asking for what He already wants to give you.

Then waiting (expecting) to receive the promise of newness and freshness from His Spirit as you go along, more each day—praying until, as the prophet Hosea said . . .

> He will come to us like the rain, like the spring rain watering the earth. (Hos. 6:3)

How does a person receive rain? Not by prying it loose from the sky but just by watching it fall, by standing in the downpour, by thanking Him for opening up the floodgates and sending what He knows we need and can't get for ourselves, yet what He so faithfully, regularly, and graciously gives.

Let's get going, then . . . with just these few little verses to get you started. Grab a pen, flip to the pages for prayer in the back of this book, and write your own prayer strategy for passion—a prayer for God to help you maintain it (if it's good) or regain it (if it's gone). Make it part *Praise*, part *Repentance*, part *Asking*, and a whole lot of *Yes*.

But don't just *read* the words you've crafted. *Pray them.* No matter if your writing is short, long, or somewhere in between, pray it as the steady, fervent desire of your will, in anticipation of seeing it become the burning desire of your heart. Because it's not just another do-better in your list of New Year's resolutions. It's a prayer strategy.

And *that's* what makes it work.

YOUR FOCUS

FIGHTING THE REAL ENEMY

If I were your enemy, I'd disguise myself and manipulate your perspectives so that you'd focus on the wrong culprit— your husband, your friend, your hurt, your finances, anything or anyone except me. Because when you zero in on the most convenient, obvious places to strike back against your problems, you get the impression you're fighting for something. Even though all you're really doing is just . . . fighting. For nothing.

Fervent prayer relies on focus.

Focus clears away dead space and clutter. It's what sharpens the images in your photographs, capturing the detail and highlights you want to remember, while pushing less important things to the background or cropping them out altogether. *Focus* minimizes distractions, lowering your risk of being blindsided. It keeps you from being preoccupied, from overlooking important facts that would've been readily obvious if you'd only been paying better attention. *Focus* protects your goals and dreams from being consumed in small bites, stolen right out from under your nose in twenty-minute segments of compromise.

And *focus* is the antenna that prayer helps to keep raised and alert, making you keenly aware if somebody's trying to play you for a fool.

And your enemy—for his strategy against you to work— is dead set on being able to succeed at just that. On fooling you. Faking you out. Pulling your eye toward a side stage on the theater platform, diverting your focus, trying to convince you that the *main* issues in your life actually originate over *there*, anywhere, or with anyone except where they really do. He wants you focused on things that are physical and visible instead of where the action really is. "Pay no attention," in other words, "to the man behind the curtain."

Reminds me of one of the more creative displays I've ever seen at the annual trunk-or-treat kids' festival a church in my neighborhood hosts during the fall. One guy connected a large, flat, wooden tabletop to the side of his pickup truck, cut five to six medium-sized holes in it, and draped it with a curtain. Sticking up through those holes was a family of wiggly, happy, hand puppets. Kids were standing in line to climb up into the truck bed to try bopping the puppets on the head with a big, cushy hammer before the figures ducked and disappeared down the hole and out of sight.

Whack-a-Mole—the church parking lot version.

One little guy, however, no more than five years old, got tired of waiting. Bored with the shenanigans, he slipped out of line, ambled around to the side of the truck for a better look, and then—for whatever curious reason—grabbed a handful of that curtain and yanked it clean off the playing surface. Suddenly, instead of six cutesy puppets swaying playfully in the evening air, there were three grown adults with both arms poking up through bare wood, a puppet on each hand, their identities immediately revealed.

Even the under-ten crowd got the message *that* night: there is something you *can't* see working underneath the surface, controlling and manipulating what you *can*.

And in Ephesians, one of my favorite books in the Bible, that's exactly what the apostle Paul tries to tell us:

> For our struggle is not against flesh and blood [what you *can* see], but against the rulers, against the powers, against the world forces of this darkness, against the spiritual forces of wickedness in the heavenly places [what you *can't* see]. (Eph. 6:12, with my additional comments)

Hear that again: Flesh and blood, skin and bones—
those aren't the places where your real struggles lie. The
identity of your real enemy, once the Bible has weighed in,
is clear as day. It's him. It's *all* him. It's *always* been him.

But in the rough-and-tumble of life's exhausting pace,
we can quickly lose touch with a passage like Ephesians
6. Even in knowing the truth, we can lose sight of where
these attacks are originating from . . . from back there,
behind the curtain. And by failing to take notice and
remember, it's not hard then to lose our cool, our temper,
and most of our self-control before we ever find our way
back to ultimate reality.

The Ephesians of Paul's day didn't need much convincing of the fact that their real problems weren't on the physical side of things. These first-century Greeks were mostly
pagan, of course, and the spirit world was very much alive in
their cognizant awareness. So as God drew men and women
to Himself from among this pantheistic culture, these early
believers in Christ were already well-schooled in the reality
of spiritual entities at play in the world. Today, however—in
Western culture, at least—our innate tendency is to *underestimate* Satan's power. Even his presence is sometimes
imagined as make-believe, no more than a phantom wear-
ing a red jumpsuit and a pitchfork, a monster hiding in the
closet. We've made him no more than a caricature instead
of the treacherous, conniving, hell-bent, personalized men-
ace he truly is. As a result, we sort of give him room to

scheme and scare at will, while we run around firing off at anyone and everyone except *him*. But if all we're doing is whacking at the nearest, most visible symptoms every time they pop their head up, we're doing two things: (1) wasting precious time and energy that ought to be reserved and refocused on the real enemy, and (2) trying to fight ferocious spiritual forces by using weapons that don't faze them in the least—weapons that aren't even designed to hurt them. So the hits just keep on coming.

Because our *focus* is all off.

And that's exactly what your real enemy is counting on.

The real enemy isn't your husband. Or your teenager. Or your brother's wife. Or your mother-in-law. Or the weather. Or the traffic. Or your sweet tooth. Or whatever powder keg of frustration really gets under your skin and sets you off before you can think straight.

The *real* enemy—the capital-E "Enemy"—

Well . . . you *know* who it is. And you simply cannot keep letting him go unchecked while you throw money and anger and logic and psychology at your problems in a vain attempt at overcoming or outsmarting them. In order to live in victory, you must call the enemy's bluff, pull the curtain back, open up your spiritual eyes, and remain continually aware of the one who's truly behind a lot of the stuff you're always blaming on your circumstances, your upbringing, your boyfriend, or whoever. Even on yourself.

In prayer you can do it differently. You can maintain this level of focus. Because *prayer*, perhaps more than anything, is meant to be an eye-opening experience.

Prayer is a reminder to yourself, as well as a declaration to the enemy, that you know he's there. That you're *on* to him. When you bring your concerns and fears and irritations to the Lord in prayer, you're aligning your weakling spirit with the full force of God's Holy Spirit. Instead of continuing to fail by taking the battle into your own hands—and taking the battle to the wrong people—you're joining instead with all the power of heaven to take your fight directly to the source of the problem. You're following the armies of the living God right into the field tent where your enemy is cooking up his craftiest designs against you, and you're busting up his strategy closet—making sure *he* knows that *you* know that you know what he's up to.

I'm not saying, now, that every bad, uncomfortable thing that enters your life is automatically oozing up from the pit of hell. Sometimes simply the nature of the world in which we live can bring "tribulation" out of the woodwork (John 16:33), and sometimes the reap-what-we-sow consequences of our own actions can put us in challenging, arduous positions (Gal. 6:7). The Bible tells us that God is sovereign enough to employ any device necessary to draw our hearts back to Him, whether He's wanting to uncover hidden sins . . . or teach us lessons in trust . . . or refine us and prepare us in whatever way He deems fit in His all-wise, all-loving mind (Judg. 3:4; James 1:2–3). But God (by contrast to the enemy) *wants* us to know He will use any measure to help us and grow us, even if it calls for the temporary pain of *those* measures. He wants us to know we can trust Him even with difficulty and discipline, or with the unavoidable happenings of life on a fallen planet because He promises to work "all things" together for our good and His purposes (Rom. 8:28).

The devil's deeds, however, are so unlike this. They're almost always accompanied by darkness and deception. Cloak and dagger. Smoke and mirrors. He "disguises himself as an angel of light" (2 Cor. 11:14). Success, to him, means stirring up discord in your home, your church, your workplace, your neighborhood, and doing it in such a way that no one's even aware he's been in the building. He knows our natural, physical response is to start coming after *each other* instead of *him*—attacking, counterattacking, pointing fingers, assigning blame—while he sits out in the driveway monitoring the clamor inside, fiendishly rubbing his hands together, admiring just how adept he is . . . and what easy targets we are.

The false ideologies of the culture (obsession with appearance, perceptions of worth, the redefinition of the family, all of it) have not been developed by chance. Don't believe it for a second. The temptations that appeal to your specific desires (and the fact that they appear at your weakest, most vulnerable moments) are not accidental. The disharmony and dysfunction that either blow up or simmer beneath your most valuable relationships are not coincidental. *None* of these things is a matter of happenstance. They are his deceptive tactics (and that of his evil entourage), being stirred up in the heavenly realm and then manifesting themselves in the physical realm.

And I say if he wants to keep pulling this stuff, then we're pulling the gloves off. And putting the armor on.

And focusing it *all* on him.

The apostle Paul, in Ephesians 6:10–11, wrote words that are worth memorizing and regularly reciting to ourselves: "Be strong in the Lord and in the strength of His might" by putting on the "full armor of God" and thereby becoming "able to stand firm against the schemes of the devil." And here they are—the needed weapons and protection for actively defeating the real enemy (vv. 14–17)—the belt of truth, the breastplate of righteousness, the shoes of gospel peace, the shield of faith, the helmet of salvation, and the sword of the Spirit, better known as the Word of God.

That's some tough stuff there. Heavy metal. But look beyond the creative, warlike imagery to see the real staying power behind each piece of battleground equipment:

- *Truth* is God's standard—the unchanging, objective benchmark of the Bible by which we govern and align our lives.

- *Righteousness* means right living—the process by which we apply this truth to our lives and, by His Spirit, produce conduct honoring and pleasing to God.

- *Peace* is the deep, inner, eternal stability the believer possesses by virtue of relationship with Jesus, a sense of balance that's not subject to external circumstance. It's also the quality that enables us to live harmoniously with others.

- *Faith* is the application of what one believes—the process of putting feet to our beliefs and living in light of it . . . in practical terms.

- *Salvation* is both our eternal security with Christ, as well as the full inheritance we've been given because of our relationship with Him. It includes our blessings, status, and identity—everything we've received that enables us to live victoriously for Him.

- *The Word of God* is His present, relevant, personal Word to us for today. The Bible may be an old Book, but God's Spirit makes it fresh, new, and alive for us.

When you resolve to use these weapons—weapons that are "not of the flesh, but divinely powerful for the destruction" of the enemy's plots (2 Cor. 10:4), you can cut him off at the pass and hit him where it hurts.

And again, the one weapon that ties this whole ensemble together, the one that activates and infuses our armor with the power of God Himself . . . is prayer. *Prayer!* "Pray at all times in the Spirit," Paul said (Eph. 6:18). The original word translated "at all times" in this verse is *kairos*, which refers to *specific* times, *precise* occasions, and *particular* events. In spiritual warfare, as we detect enemy activity and deploy the various pieces of armor, our prayers need to be fervent and specific, strategic and personal, tied to the specific needs arising at that specific occasion. *That's* the kind of prayer that energizes the armor of God for maximum effectiveness, prayed "with all perseverance and petition for all the saints" (v. 18). Pray for *you*. Pray for *me*. Pray for *all* of us, he says, that we'll live with the curtain pulled back, able to spot the real enemy when we see him. And through the bold, mighty name of Jesus, pray that we'll live with our armor on and not let Satan's otherworldly forces wreak their havoc in *this* house, in *this* heart, on *this* day.

That's called being *focused* and *strategic* in prayer.

And it works, I'm telling you. Physical weapons may work in physical battles. Stuff like . . . trying harder, getting up earlier, moving across town to a new neighborhood, making him sleep on the sofa, giving her a piece of your mind. But this ain't no physical battle we're dealing with, no matter how much you may wish it to be, no matter how much better you'd feel if life was all five-senses and manageable. We are at *spiritual war.* So we need spiritual weapons.

And in prayer—in Jesus, with these weapons—guess what: *you win!* In fact, you've already *won!* Victory is already yours. Through Christ, Satan has already been:

- disarmed and embarrassed (Col. 2:15)
- overruled (Eph. 1:20–22)
- mastered (Phil. 2:9–11)
- rendered powerless (Heb. 2:14)
- all his hard work destroyed (1 John 3:8)

Now you can just walk in that victory and claim what is rightfully yours. Dressed in the armor of Ephesians 6 and committed to the practice that activates our spiritual power—*prayer*—all you need is one bullet, trained on one enemy, tracing his one path as he skirts around corners and slithers up through the ductwork, finding any little rat hole he can squeeze through.

Nice try, devil. But your tricks are no good here. We're shutting you down. Shutting you out. Praying with full voice where you can hear us loud and clear.

Now hear this—

Get. *Gone.*

Call to Prayer

Some of the Scriptures I'm about to share with you are the kind that help rip down the veil of secrecy between the physical world and the spiritual world. They're almost like 3-D glasses that you wear into a movie theater to help you see the film the way it's been created. Without the special lenses everything looks fuzzy and out of focus. Flat. Distorted. You *think* you sort of see it but not really—because the naked eye is not able to process the visual information of a 3-D movie and put it together in a usable form in our brains. It's all just blurry. A headache. But when you slide those glasses on, you'll see what you were always intended to see. The whole world suddenly comes alive. The villain is *right there*, in your face. Can't miss him. The texture and layering and perspective—ahhh, so *this* is what it's supposed to look like. *This* is how it really is.

Once the unseen enemy is exposed and comes into clear view, you can lift your focus away from the people, places, and events that have always seemed like the main culprits of your human dramas and stop wasting your energy on methods that are ineffective and, honestly, flat-out exhausting. Instead, you can lift your eyes to Jesus—who has always known who the real enemy is, and who knows this so-called enemy doesn't have a pinkie's worth of power against the One who clipped that imposter's wings on Calvary. And because He did, Satan doesn't stand a real chance against you now. Not after that.

So build a prayer strategy against the one who "comes only to steal and kill and destroy" but who meets His match in the matchless One who came that we might have life "and have it abundantly" (John 10:10). Personalize your prayer by asking

God to help you pull back the curtain today—and every single day—so you can see when the devil is behind the argument, the frustration, the anger, the discord, the falsehood, the insecurity, the fear. Ask Him to help you take your attention and emotional energy off the people and circumstances where you've been directing them up till now and refocus them. Let verses like these be your guide as you write . . .

> I am convinced that nothing can ever separate us from God's love. Neither death nor life, neither angels nor demons, neither our fears for today nor our worries about tomorrow—not even the powers of hell can separate us from God's love. No power in the sky above or in the earth below—indeed, nothing in all creation will ever be able to separate us from the love of God that is revealed in Christ Jesus our Lord. (Rom. 8:38–39 NLT)

～

> He is far above any ruler or authority or power or leader or anything else—not only in this world but also in the world to come. (Eph. 1:21 NLT)

～

> God highly exalted Him, and bestowed on Him the name which is above every name, so that at the name of Jesus every knee will bow, of those who are

in heaven and on earth and under the earth, and that every tongue will confess that Jesus Christ is Lord, to the glory of God the Father. (Phil. 2:9–11)

〜

I will exalt you, LORD, for you rescued me.
You refused to let my enemies triumph over me.
    (Ps. 30:1 NLT)

〜

Do not rejoice over me, O my enemy.
Though I fall I will rise;
Though I dwell in darkness, the LORD is a light for
    me. (Mic. 7:8)

〜

Though I walk in the midst of trouble, You will
    revive me;
You will stretch forth Your hand against the wrath
    of my enemies,
And Your right hand will save me. (Ps. 138:7)

〜

By this I know that You delight in me:
my enemy does not shout in triumph over me.
    (Ps. 41:11 HCSB)

≪≫

Let God arise, let His enemies be scattered,
And let those who hate Him flee before Him.
   (Ps. 68:1)

≪≫

Lead us not into temptation, but deliver us from
evil: For thine is the kingdom, and the power, and
the glory, for ever. (Matt. 6:13 KJV)

≪≫

The Lord is faithful, and He will strengthen and
protect you from the evil one. (2 Thess. 3:3)

Truly, our enemy is going to pay for what He's done and
is doing to us, for daring to pick on the children of God.

So whether with Scriptures like these or with others
that the Holy Spirit calls to your attention, take a stab at
writing down your own prayer strategy to help you remember the name of your *real* enemy and—most importantly—
remember the Name above all names.

- *Praise:* Thank Him for reigning in power and supply-
  ing you with the weapons of victory.
- *Repentance:* Admit where you've been angry and
  distracted, fighting all the wrong people.

- *Asking:* Ask for courage, for discernment, for patience, for diligence, for laser-like focus.
- *Yes:* Because the Lord is with you, and He will fight the real enemy through you.

And be encouraged by what one prophet of God told the people of God on the eve of battle centuries ago . . .

Thus says the LORD to you, "Do not fear or be dismayed because of this great multitude, for the battle is not yours but God's. . . . Station yourselves, stand and see the salvation of the LORD on your behalf, O Judah and Jerusalem. Do not fear or be dismayed; tomorrow go out and face them, for the LORD is with you. (2 Chron. 20:15, 17)

Your Identity

Remembering Who You Are

If I were your enemy, I'd devalue your strength and magnify your insecurities until they dominate how you see yourself, disabling and disarming you from fighting back, from being free, from being who God has created you to be. I'd work hard to ensure that you never realize what God has given you so you'll doubt the power of God within you.

It was a tragic scene.

Abby, a nineteen-year-old college sophomore, was returning home with four other friends on a spring break outing to Disneyland, when the SUV in which she was riding experienced a blowout that turned into a fatal accident. Two of the girls were ejected from the car and died on the scene. Abby was identified as one of them.

As word reached the families back in Arizona—two girls dead, three critically injured—typical parental worry over a college road trip turned to unspeakable grief. Abby's parents spent the next few days combing through the shock and horror, planning the details of their daughter's funeral while three other parents prayed for their own children's recovery, some of whose bruises and swelling made them almost hard to recognize as they lay in the hospital.

On Saturday, however, six days after the accident, hospital officials informed two of the families that there had been a horrible mistake. Two of the girls, who bore a striking resemblance, had been misidentified. Parents who'd been sitting by the bedside of a young woman they believed to be their daughter were told the staggering news: she wasn't their daughter after all. Their daughter had actually died in the accident. And Abby's parents? They were given news they could have never imagined receiving . . .

Abby wasn't dead. She was alive.

The initial shock of what they were hearing turned to disbelief. Disbelief then turned to joy. But the joy was mingled, too, with anger—anger that they'd been forced to live for six days in agony because of a reality that wasn't true, a grief that they had no need to feel or experience.

It all boiled down to a case of mistaken identity.

The enemy wants *you* to suffer from a case of mistaken identity. Makes his job a whole lot easier. And makes your defenses a lot weaker. He's working overtime to keep your identity masked, to keep the truth from coming out—that you are indeed alive and free and empowered by God's own Spirit to fight victoriously against him. He'd rather conspire to keep you in a constant state of mourning, grieving over who you *wish* you were, instead of relishing who you really *are*, exacerbated by insecurity and crippled by self-doubt.

That's why he doesn't want you praying—not *fervently*—because fervent prayer keeps your true identity in focus. Reminds us of who we really are and taps into the power we really have in Christ.

This authentic identity is possibly quite a bit different from the one you perceive when you look at yourself in the mirror each day, or when you're fidgeting through an awkward social encounter, or when you're sizing yourself up against the well-dressed accomplishments of other friends, other church members, even (and you know it's true) even total strangers. It's also not the identity your enemy wants in your head when he's moving strategically against you, when he's maneuvering himself into attack position. He wants you lifeless, disengaged, brainwashed into believing you have nothing of value to offer.

That's why he doesn't want your nose in the Word or your knees on the hardwood. Because that's where the light comes on. That's where you find out the good news, perhaps the surprisingly euphoric news—that you are alive, fully equipped to stand firm against him. "Formerly darkness," the Bible says, yes. Formerly. At one time. But now "Light in the Lord" . . . "children of Light" . . . able through Christ to produce "the fruit of the Light" (Eph. 5:8–9).

That's why Paul, in his colossal letter to the Ephesians, came roaring out of the starting gate with one reminder after another of the spiritual blessings we've been given, purely as the result of Christ's love toward us, commensurate with the enormous value He's placed on us. I almost hesitate to list them for fear you'll skim over them, feeling all too familiar with them, knowing them already. But I'm asking you to soak them into your soul. Let Paul's identity sketch from Ephesians 1 embed itself into the floorboard of your deepest insecurities. You are:

- equipped through Christ with "every spiritual blessing" (v. 3)
- chosen in Him "before the foundation of the world" (v. 4)
- regarded as "holy and blameless before Him" (v. 4)
- adopted through the "kind intention of His will" (v. 5)
- redeemed and forgiven, "lavished" with grace (vv. 7–8)
- recipients of a glorious "inheritance" in heaven (v. 11)
- secured forever by "the Holy Spirit of promise" (vv. 13–14)

I could go on. Like Paul does. This list is just one quick sampling from one chapter, from one book of the Bible, from one small corner of God's blessing barn, poured out like a thousand Christmas mornings—*every* morning— every time you wake up to the partly cloudy forecast of a new day.

But what I love most—and what the devil seriously hopes you don't notice—is that Paul didn't just deliver all this spiritual material like a class lecture, writing stray bits of information on the board, stuff you might do well to remember for the next big test coming up. No, right in the middle of Paul's dictation, notice how his prepared mono- logue (around verses 15 and 16) begins blending almost seamlessly into a prayer. You think he's just talking, and then just like that . . . he's praying. Praying that our eyes would be open to really, fully *see* and recognize who we truly are. Praying that we would:

- receive a "spirit of wisdom" from the Father (v. 17)
- be enlightened to grasp the "hope of His calling" (v. 18)
- recognize the "riches of the glory of His inheritance" (v. 18)
- know the "surpassing greatness of His power" toward us (v. 19)
- realize we are "seated [with] Him . . . in heavenly places" (v. 20)

- and that even though we *were* "dead," He has given us life (2:5)

There's strategy to this combination of the Word and prayer. From Scripture we receive written proof of what God has done for us, what He's created us and called us and empowered us into becoming. Then in prayer we cooperate with Him to stamp these truths repeatedly into our hearts. And then, more than that, we access them and engage them and draw down their power into our everyday experience.

In prayer we watch words on a page turn a new leaf in us, both in our hearts and in our day-to-day living. In prayer we feel a bolstering that energizes us with holy confidence. In prayer we set off like trailblazers, carving fresh neural pathways within our brains, transforming the way we think of ourselves, receiving and believing our true identity—the one that was stamped on us the moment we ran to the foot of the cross. Pray long and hard enough, and not only do we realize we're indeed alive, but we become angry—furious!—that we've been in mourning for so long, saddened by a tragedy whose outcome was totally misreported to us.

As adopted daughters of the living God, if we're not strategically praying in accordance with who our Maker and Redeemer says we are, if we aren't calling ourselves by name according to that list from Ephesians, serving the devil notice that we know (like *he* knows) who we really are, we'll always be subject to his attempts at devaluing us. We'll downplay our real strength. We'll hate our bodies, highlight our weaknesses, cringe with insecurities, and constantly view ourselves as "less than" by comparison with others. He'll diffuse our power simply by downplaying our true position.

If he can get you to believe his lies, you won't feel equipped or entitled to stand up against him. You'll be weak and helpless, and then he can run roughshod over you and over the things and people you love. The farther he can separate your practical reality from your true, living reality, he can wedge himself into the space between the two and short-circuit the free-flowing effectiveness of your influence as a wife, a mom, a friend, a daughter, a sister—all the relationships where God has placed you to be a light of His grace, His power, His love, His well-placed confidence.

That's why you and I need to be praying—to keep the truth about our real identity in constant, unbroken focus before us.

The *truth*.

One of the pieces of spiritual armor supplied to us as believers (Eph. 6:14) centers in on this issue precisely. It is what's commonly known as the "belt of truth." More accurately, based on the history of what a first-century soldier's gear was like, think of it as sort of a *girdle*, worn close around the body, with all his other pieces of armor tucked into it and held together by it. Underwear, kind of.

A foundation garment. The first thing a soldier would put on before going into battle.

Truth—God's standard and viewpoint about us—must come first in our hearts and minds if we want to be effective in battle against the enemy. We need to put it on as our foundational garment and then reorient everything else around it. Before we accessorize with trendy add-ons, before we drive off into the day, artificially covered by an outfit that only masks any of the lies the enemy is deceiving us into believing about ourselves, we should start with the underpinnings of truth, secured through prayer by the declarations of God's Word. Because unless our whole ensemble is framed around this undergarment, we're not really suited for spiritual battle. We're not dressed for the occasion. Not ready for what's coming.

That's why the apostle Paul prayed so fervently that the true identity of those first-century believers would be unveiled in their hearts. Hear that again: He wasn't asking God to make sure the early believers *received* these things. They already *had* them. He was praying they'd *realize* they already had them.

It wasn't a shopping list; it was a packing list. They didn't need to buy them, didn't need to manufacture them. They just needed to recognize that they had access to them and could now receive them as their own to take full advantage of them.

Because sometimes, even with a closet full of clothes, we can look in and think there's nothing to wear. But look again. Through the eyes of truth. And you might finally see that not only have you been given what you need but a whole lot more.

A whole, *whole* lot more.

Perhaps, again, the story of an experience between the Old Testament prophet Elisha and one of his servants can help us understand what we fail to see when we're not looking at our lives through the lens of God's truth.

Immediately on the heels of the floating ax head miracle in 2 Kings 6—which we talked about a few chapters ago—the Bible tells of war breaking out between a neighboring nation (the Arameans) and the people of Israel. While the king of Aram was working out his attack strategy, the Lord kept tipping off Elisha to the king's intentions and movements. Then Elisha would deliver these divinely accurate spy reports to the king of Israel, who would redeploy his soldiers into perfectly placed, perfectly timed position to defend themselves.

Drove the king of Aram crazy—crazy enough to go hunting the mole among his ranks who was obviously working as a double agent, feeding Aramean intel to their opponent. But his enraged questioning eventually led him to the truth—that it was Elisha and his bedroom talks with God that were the real source behind these tactical leaks. And by the time the king surrounded the city where Elisha was located, intending to take him out by force, an even greater truth was about to be revealed.

The prophet's attendant woke up early that morning, went outside to stretch his legs or something, and—*whoa!*—the whole place was teeming with horses and chariots and the clink of sharpened artillery, each of them assembled for a surgical strike. The servant ran back inside and—sounding a lot like the guy with the lost ax—started going all to pieces, stammering to his boss about their imminent danger.

Elisha, cool as ever, told him not to worry because "those who are with us are more than those who are with them" (2 Kings 6:16). Then setting the same lifestyle tone that Paul would exhibit so naturally in Ephesians 1, his next words to his servant were not a list of next steps to follow or a battle strategy to implement but a prayer to the Father: "O LORD, I pray, open his eyes that he may see" (v. 17).

When the terrified servant turned back around after hearing Elisha's prayer, what he saw was not the *physical* reality of fire-breathing army troops itching to attack but rather the *spiritual* reality of a mountainside filled to the brim with angelic chariots of fire, surrounding, protecting, and preventing any warrior of the Aramean army from taking a single shot or making even one step toward them.

Prayer made him *aware* of all the resources and strength and protection that God had already placed on their side. Without this renewed perspective he was already defeated before the battle had even begun . . . before the day had even started.

That's what the enemy wants. He wants you living in a state of defeat. Your defenses down. Your resolve weak and flimsy. Surrendering to an army of insecurities and misdiagnosis instead of courageously thriving in the sophisticated security of your identity in Christ.

Makes you wonder, then, why all we often tend to see when we look at ourselves are . . . flaws, inadequacies, failures, weaknesses. And sure, many of those things are really there. Left to our own devices, we really *aren't* able to take it all on, not without help. But these difficulties and imperfections that can discourage us so desperately—the ones the devil wants to present as the *sum total* of our reality—are actually only a *part* of the battlefield. And that's the part that is primed to display God's glory. No matter what is against you, it is no match for the power and authority He's given you access to. There may be armies standing against you, but they're only waiting to become an unwitting witness to the overcoming power of God and the overriding ocean of His grace.

And prayer will *open your eyes* so you can see it—can see who you really are, that you are alive indeed, and that divine resources and riches and solutions are on your side, assets that make you "more than victorious" through the sheer size of His love (Rom. 8:37 HCSB).

This is the belt of truth.

Now. Put. It. On.

CALL TO PRAYER

I wish we were sitting together over coffee and being
uncharacteristically honest with each other. I'd share with
you about how I often struggle to lift myself out of the doldrums of insecurity. About how strategic and consistently
prayerful I'm forced to be in reminding myself that those
flaws and weaknesses the enemy is hell-bent on accentuat-
ing are not more important or powerful than the strengths
and resources I now have in Christ.

My struggle is the same as yours—like most every other
woman at one point or another in her life.

The enemy has been telling us for so long that we're no
good, washed-up, underequipped, incompetent, insignifi-
cant, unlovable, and not quite up to par. He's been brain-
washing us, one feminine soul at a time. But now we both
know the truth. We can see clearly that he's been lying for
the purpose of keeping us from even trying to put up a good
fight against his planned attacks. *But no more.* We're on to
him. And like the family who found out that their beloved
little girl was still alive after six long days and nights of grief,
we're excited, yes, but also angry to hear the news. Angry
that we've been misled and that our emotions have been
tampered with.

And now we're ready to take that holy indignation into
battle, on our knees, in prayer. We are fully alive and on the
path to healing and wholeness. Our story isn't even close to

being over. We are already seated in heavenly places. We're fully functional with weapons our enemy has no answer for. We are loved by God from before time began (Matt. 25:34), endowed already with the eternal Spirit of God (2 Cor. 1:22), and forgiven of even our most shameful sins (Rom. 4:7–8). If you can't believe He'd do that for you, at least believe He's done it as a testimony to the greatness of His name (Ps. 79:9) because He's God and He likes to show it. That "head and not the tail" business from Deuteronomy 28:13? God has already seen to it that the only "tail" in this real-life drama is the one who's destined to be thrown— head, tail, and all—into the "lake of fire and brimstone" (Rev. 20:10). Not you.

Not. You.

Not. Ever.

Because you are His . . . and He is yours.

Now build a prayer strategy using these passages (and others from this chapter) as a backdrop to remind yourself of this truth every day for the rest of your life.

> God is so rich in mercy, and he loved us so much, that even though we were dead because of our sins, he gave us life when he raised Christ from the dead. (It is only by grace that you have been saved!) For he raised us from the dead along with Christ and seated us with him in the heavenly realms because we are united with Christ Jesus. (Eph. 2:4–6 NLT)

⚬

I also clothed you with embroidered cloth and put sandals of porpoise skin on your feet; and I wrapped you with fine linen and covered you with silk. I adorned you with ornaments, put bracelets on your hands and a necklace around your neck. I also put a ring in your nostril, earrings in your ears and a beautiful crown on your head. . . . So you were exceedingly beautiful and advanced to royalty. (Ezek. 16:10–13)

⚬

As many as received Him, to them He gave the right to become children of God, even to those who believe in His name, who were born, not of blood nor of the will of the flesh nor of the will of man, but of God. (John 1:12–13)

⚬

We are His workmanship, created in Christ Jesus for good works, which God prepared beforehand so that we would walk in them. (Eph. 2:10)

⚬

For you have not received a spirit of slavery leading to fear again, but you have received a spirit of adoption as sons by which we cry out 'Abba! Father!' The Spirit Himself testifies with our spirit that we are children of God, and if children, heirs also, heirs of God and fellow heirs with Christ, if indeed we suffer with Him so that we may also be glorified with Him. (Rom. 8:15–17)

⸏⸐

Look to the rock from which you were hewn
And to the quarry from which you were dug.
    (Isa. 51:1)

⸏⸐

The LORD has taken you and brought you out of the iron furnace, from Egypt, to be a people for His own possession. (Deut. 4:20)

⸏⸐

Behold, I have engraved you on the palms of my hands; your walls are continually before me. (Isa. 49:16 ESV)

⸏⸐

For God, who said, "Light shall shine out of darkness," is the One who has shone in our hearts to give the Light of the knowledge of the glory of God in the face of Christ. But we have this treasure in earthen vessels, so that the surpassing greatness of the power will be of God and not from ourselves. (2 Cor. 4:6–7)

⁓

You are a chosen race, a royal priesthood, a holy nation, a people for God's own possession, so that you may proclaim the excellencies of Him who has called you out of darkness into His marvelous light. (1 Pet. 2:9)

⁓

Now to Him who is able to keep you from stumbling, and to make you stand in the presence of His glory blameless with great joy, to the only God our Savior, through Jesus Christ our Lord, be glory, majesty, dominion and authority, before all time and now and forever. Amen. (Jude 24–25)

STRATEGY 4

Your Family

Fortifying the Lives
of Those You Love

If I were your enemy, *I'd seek to disintegrate your family and destroy every member of it. I'd want to tear away at your trust and unity and turn everyone's love inward on themselves. I would make sure your family didn't look anything like it's supposed to. Because then people would look at your Christian marriage, your Christian kids, and see you're no different, no stronger than anybody else—that God, underneath it all, really doesn't change anything.*

My husband, Jerry, and I (we'd both readily admit) had a *terrible* second year of marriage. We fought early and often, long and hard. Two people so young, with so little in the bank of shared experiences with which to accumulate much ammunition. . . . Yet we still seemed to find plenty of it to go to battle with. And battle, we did. Against each other. All the time.

But we made it through by the skin of our gritted teeth. And the tough patches we endured, once we settled back down, only seemed to make us better. Closer. More committed. More complete. Fourteen years later, three kids later, we seemed to be fully hitting our stride as a family of five. We still had stuff to deal with, of course, like everybody does. But for the most part? All good. Happy.

Then came last year.

With my family's blessing I had accepted, much to even my own surprise, a part in a major faith-based film. I was shocked to be invited to participate, shocked that I was willing to risk saying yes, and shocked even more, after the directors saw my acting abilities, that they still wanted me to take the role. Took me about as far out of my comfort zone as this girl had been in a long, long time, maybe ever. The movie, as you probably know by now, is on the theme of *prayer*—the power of strategic prayer, the kind of prayer power God can activate in His people, and specifically the kind of prayer that can rescue a family before it careens off a cliff of near certain destruction.

The directors of the film wrote me a long e-mail before shooting began, filling me in on details to help me prepare for what was ahead. And among their many notes was a warning. They wanted to make me aware of Satan's penchant for targeting the people who'd been involved in their previous films and how he'd taken aim at the areas of their personal lives that were connected to the message of that movie. Since this particular project was on the theme of prayer and family, they encouraged me to be vigilant about praying for my own family, praying against any assignments the enemy may have trained against us.

Soon summer arrived. We packed our bags and moved to another state to begin a couple months of filming. I was the novice on set—didn't know what to expect as far as all the acting and directing and moviemaking were involved. But even having been forewarned, I didn't fully realize how that summer of on-site shooting would affect some of the dynamics in my family. Gosh, we were just having fun in our new surroundings, soaking up the fresh adventure of it, not really thinking about the unique set of stressors placed on all of us—being away from home, out of our element, out of our usual rhythms. But pretty soon the slightest things would set off a disagreement, a misunderstanding. Hot feelings. Short fuses. By the time we made it through our final wrap on the film set, we were exhausted, not just physically but relationally.

OK, freeze here. Get this picture of what was happening in our family at the time and how it contrasted with the message of the movie we were involved in portraying. Can't you see the enemy's strategy at work? *Of course* he would want to turn up the background noise to try complicating the work we were doing in expressing God's truth for a global audience. *Of course* he would want, if possible, to water down this important message by dismantling the relationships of the people participating in it—just as we'd been told to expect.

So since we knew who was behind the tension, we made the deliberate choice to stop fighting with each other and to fight instead with that doggoned enemy. We vigilantly asked God to make our marriage and family (and the families of all those involved in the film) bulletproof against these incessant attacks.

Too much was at stake. It was a big deal.

But you know what? *It's always a big deal.* All of our marriages and families are a huge deal. Yours *and* mine. They're *all* that big of a deal . . . because each one is a billboard for the eternal, unchangeable love story between God and humankind. Each of their successes or failures is of great importance, both in *God's* eyes and, therefore, in our *enemy's* eyes.

So he targets them. All of them. He targets our role as wives, targets our husbands, and targets our children. He brings dissension, infuses tension, unravels our sense of peace with disunity. Because ultimately he wants to destroy our families—*all* of our families—so that the billboard message they're designed to project to the world is a picture that is, at best, laughable.

Now if you're a single woman, thinking you might just flip ahead to the next chapter since this one doesn't apply to you, think again. There's more that pertains to you on this subject matter than you may realize. We're all a part of it, married or not, or just not married yet. We need everybody praying—even for a marriage and family like yours that may be still to come in the future.

Here's why: According to Scripture, the number-one purpose of marriage—more than even the unique, time-honored partnership it creates between a man and woman, more than even the conceiving and raising of children, more than any Prince Charming fairy tale in any little girl's head—is how it represents the mystery of the gospel in active, living form.

That's what a beloved professor of mine, Dr. Dwight Pentecost (who'd also been a professor to my father decades earlier) said to Jerry and me in a typewritten letter that I still treasure in a keepsake box of wedding memories. "I scarcely need remind you," he wrote, "that marriage was instituted by God to be an object lesson to the world of the relationship of a believer to Himself. Each of you will play a significant role in living out this lesson."

A man chooses a bride, loves her, makes a covenant with her, and gives himself completely to her. The woman responds by receiving his love, surrendering to him, entering into this covenant bond with him, and becoming one flesh with him. It's not a *perfect* representation, of course, since the best marriage we can possibly make on earth still involves a pair of fallen, broken people. But in its deepest sense, at its deepest level, this primary human relationship between husband and wife is meant to be a living witness to others of the love of Christ for His church (Eph. 5:22–33).

Marriage stands for the creation of unity among two people who were once separated in every way before love reached out and found the other—the way God reached out and found us, and covenanted with us, and loved us, and despite who we are, despite what we're like, *still* loves us. This image, more than almost anything, is exactly what the enemy wants to denigrate.

When Scripture counsels husbands to love and lead their wives, even when it counsels us wives to submit to our husbands—[gulp!]—the ultimate motivation for these lofty directives is not just so we'll get along better on the weekends but that our homes will reflect on earth the order of God's relationship with us. Husbands are to love their wives "just as Christ also loved the church and gave Himself up for her" (Eph. 5:25). Wives are to submit to their husbands "as the church submits to Christ" (v. 24 NLT).

Again, big deal, all around. Much bigger deal than we thought.

So when you and I begin feeling pressure and tension and splintering and conflict at home, when little trifling things start bunching together to become this one big thing—when the nitpicking turns into bickering; the bickering into outbursts; the outbursts into rude, below-the-belt unkindness and bitterness; the bitterness into slow, seething pullbacks of silence and isolation—is it just your husband being terrible? Acting awful? Is it just you being overly sensitive, slow to relinquish a foothold of cherished, hard-fought ground? Is it just your child pulling away into isolation or overt rebellion? Is it just all of you going to your own rooms—disconnected, disjointed, fragmented?

No, it bears all the marks of an outside enemy—one who *hangs* around your family but isn't *part* of your family. *He's* the one who wants your marriage to suffer. *He's* the one who wants your home to be a dueling battleground. *He's* the one who's most invested in sending each of you out the door every day vulnerable and susceptible to temptation, needy for the unconditional love and acceptance you're supposed to be giving and receiving from each other.

But is *he* the one on the receiving end of your frustration? Is *he* the one you're splattering with juicy comebacks, spoken with disgust against the inside glass of your windshield while you're driving down the road, rehearsing the script for your next altercation? Because the fact is, *he's* most likely the one who's pulled the wool over your eyes, fooling you with a crafty bait and switch, leading you to focus all your indignation on your man or your kid instead.

He wants you miserable and exhausted and joyless and undone. He wants that picture of the gospel—the one you call your marriage and your family—he wants it tarnished. Ripped up. Smeared in the mud of failure. Held up as fresh meat from the kill. Turning you against each other and tearing everybody in half. As much as the Father loves and embodies unity, your enemy loves and embodies division. Wherever discord is present, he's never too far away. And as most of us sadly know from far too much personal experience, no wounds cut as deep or cleave us at the core of our existence more than the wounds we receive at the hands of our family.

You'd better believe he wants a piece of that action.

But maybe he wasn't counting on this: a woman who'd had enough, enough to start taking some *prayer* action. For her marriage, for her husband, for her children—for all her family.

So here we go. This is it. Bring your family issues right up to the line here, and let's get some stuff out in the open. Let's get specific. Let's put a bead on the bull's-eye where the real source of your family strife and discomfort and unmet needs are originating from, and let's show him the kind of resistance that a steady dose of prayer is able to exact against his demolition plans.

Is it your marriage? Then quit trying to be the Holy Spirit in your relationship, responsible for poking and prodding that husband of yours until he finally sees things the same way you see them. I'll admit I spent some of my first years as a married woman convinced that my primary spiritual gift in life was to change Jerry . . . in *Jesus' name!* It's taken me nearly two decades to begin realizing I was wrong. Changing Jerry, as it turns out, is *not* my spiritual gift. Nowhere in 1 Corinthians 12, or anywhere else in Scripture where the divinely infused gifts of God's Spirit are listed, does "improving thy husband" appear as even a footnoted selection. And if we didn't know this to be the case from its obvious absence among the catalog of spiritual gifts, haven't we all discovered from exhausting experience that the Holy Spirit all by Himself can do a much better job of it than we ever could?

No, our job—my job, your job—is not to change that man but to respect him and then leave the rest to the Lord. When you do this, you're not letting him off the hook at all—you're just leaving him to God. You're also well on your way to discovering something else: he's likely not the *only* one who needs to do some changing. In fact, he probably isn't the one (at *my* house, at least) who needs changing the most. The more you pray for your husband, the more the Spirit will shine a spotlight on the places in your own heart and actions that need a bit of work too.

The only effective way to fight in marriage is to pray. The way to see the real truth behind whatever's happening in this whole situation of yours . . . is to pray. The way to get the wheels moving again that have clogged up or perhaps totally come off . . . is to pray. Prayer is how we isolate the real problems. And prayer is how we get up behind those problems and attack them at the roots. It's how we isolate the real enemy. It's how we keep him on his heels and off our man.

And prayer is also how God gets through to *us*, even while we're praying for our husband, convincing us that maybe what our husband needs most right now is for his wife to become a soft, safe place for him to land, rather than a prickly, nagging source of contention that only agitates him and makes things worse.

So even if things are going pretty well for you right now, even if you don't have a lot to complain about or feel upset over, the enemy is still there, whether in full-on attack mode or lurking in wait for the next possible opportunity to infiltrate. So pray. And pray fervently.

Is it your children? The Bible says our children are "like arrows in the hand of a warrior" (Ps. 127:4). We raise them up to shoot them out into the culture, bearing the image of Christ to the world. Sounds again, then, like a place that would qualify as a major area of concern for an enemy who doesn't want any vestige of Christian valor and virtue running loose out there where . . . I don't know, they might take bold stands of faith and influence around their college friends. Might pastor a church or run a business or become involved in missions and ministry opportunities that honor Christ and actively serve hundreds of people. Worst of all, they might marry and raise up a whole *other* generation of little Christ followers, keeping your family burning red hot on enemy radar long beyond your lifetime, spinning up a legacy of faith that spirals forward undaunted into the future.

Your enemy can't be having any of that, now, can he?

So don't be surprised when he starts coming after your kids. And don't think it's all because they're being headstrong or peer dependent or careless or lazy. Satan knows the parts of their character—both their strengths and their weaknesses—where he can worm in and try stunting their growth, their potential, and their confidence.

One of my sons, for example, has always been prone toward fear and anxiety. Ever since he was a small child, he's shown a noticeable bent toward this kind of emotional response to external stimuli. Knowing this—spotting this— I've been very specific in praying for him, *out loud* over him, even when he was just a baby. I've routinely asked the Holy Spirit to instill courage within him, to be a wall of protection against the enemy's attempts to exploit my son in this sensitive area.

Three or four years ago, night after night, he started seeing something he described as a man in his room. It couldn't *really* be a man in there, of course. The outside doors and windows were locked. Nobody was getting inside. Part of me wanted to write it off as nothing, tell him to go back to sleep and not worry about it. But he was able to tell me in rather striking detail what this "man" looked like, where he was standing in relation to my son's bed, how paralyzing it felt when he sensed this presence in the room, as if a heavy blanket had fallen on him, suffocating him.

That did it. I started to pray over him even more specifically, to pray over their room while the boys were away, to command this spirit of fear to leave my son alone in the name of Jesus. One day in particular when this issue seemed to be reaching a climax of intensity, I stormed into that bedroom like a rocket. I paced the floor, I quoted Scripture, I posted passages on the wall, I laid hands on the doorposts and window ledges.

And I'm not joking here, that was the last day my boy ever mentioned that man. As far as I know, he's never been bothered by it since to that degree or in that precise way.

Let the enemy run roughshod over my kids? No way. And I have a strong feeling you won't allow him to do it to yours either.

An enemy is after your children, I'm telling you. Believe it. Know it. But most important, *deal with it*—by tunneling deep into your prayer closet and fighting back with every parental and spiritual weapon at your disposal.

Is it an issue with other family members? Perhaps your most pressing family issues right now pertain not to your husband, not to your children, but to other members of your extended family who are unsaved, feeling the brunt of enemy attack on themselves, or who are participating (intentionally or unintentionally) with the enemy's designs on you as their daughter, their sister, their cousin, their daughter-in-law, whatever. The forms that these sorts of conflict can take are as numerous as the number of people involved in them. But just as much as the devil loves stirring up trouble in churches, he loves stirring up trouble in families. He knows it's a Christian witness killer, an energy zapper, a time eater, a relationship destroyer. The amount of senseless hurt and distraction he can cause per square inch in your family is one of his most desirable economies of scale. He can do more damage with less effort by attacking us here, within these relationships, than in any other context. But if we're wise, we can use his own geometry against him, putting prayer into effect in places where we're close enough to touch the very people involved. Then as God's Spirit does His work in us and in these situations, the others in our family will be standing close enough to watch it all happen in real time, to see the kinds of change and impact our prayers are able to accomplish.

Again, *if you're a single woman,* don't think this chapter doesn't apply to you. If you're wise, you'll discern that it most certainly does. Praying for your mate shouldn't begin when you've walked down the aisle. It should start now, before you've been on the first date or even know his first name. Pray for the man God may be positioning as your future husband. Pray that he'll be set ablaze with love for Christ and a heart for leading you well and making your marriage a devoted priority. Pray that God would guard his friendships and those who will influence the path he is taking even right now. Pray that his passions would be attuned with an authentic faith, that his purity would be a matter of deep commitment, and that God would superintend the circumstances that bring the two of you together . . . all in His perfect plan and His perfect timing.

If you don't have children of your own, pray for the little ones (nieces, nephews, neighbors) who are in your life and whom God brings specifically to your attention. And yes, begin praying now for the child or children He may entrust to you at a later time, through whatever means He leads you to take. I once knew a guy who began setting aside $100 a month for his children when he was in his mid-twenties— and he didn't even marry until he was in his early thirties! He was preparing a nest of security *in advance* for his child to be born into. Prayer allows you to do the same thing in the spiritual realm, to prepare an environment of spiritual security and the first stirring of a family legacy before your child is even stirring in the womb. Can you imagine what a gift it could be, years from now, for your children to see your handwritten, fervent prayers for them before they even took their first breath?

The family is one of the key axis points of God's purposes on earth. And *your* family, at the point of *your* sphere of influence, is a major component of what He is doing right here where you live. In order to make sure you're fully cooperating with Him and with the enormous opportunity embodied in your family structure and its people, they need you to not be on their backs, not be up in their faces, but be down on your knees.

Assume a new fighting position.

CALL TO PRAYER

If for some reason you've only been skimming through these early chapters so far, not really stopping to turn to the pages in the back of the book and formulate your own strategies for praying against Satan's attacks on your passion, your focus, your identity, I hope this will be the place where you really do take time to pull off to the side, break away from just trying to finish another book that you started, and spend some concentrated effort in crafting specific, strategic, personalized prayer approaches for your family. Person by person. Name by name. The stakes are simply too high not to do it.

I think we've all resorted at one time or another to the roll-call system for covering our family in prayer. Lord, bless my husband; Lord, bless my kids; be with my aunt and uncle in Ohio; be with my dad and his knee replacement rehab; be with my brother who's looking for work. Quick. Easy. Over and done. Better than totally ignoring them perhaps, but hardly a satisfying confidence that you're going all out, participating mightily with God in their future, their provision, or their rescue.

"Beloved," the apostle John wrote, "I pray that in all respects you may prosper and be in good health, just as your soul prospers" (3 John 2). "May He give you what your heart desires and fulfill your whole purpose" (Ps. 20:4 HCSB). The Scripture is full of eternal truths, made even more relevant when framed against the context of your family's life, specific needs, and dilemmas.

There are verses and counsel related to how a wife treats, blesses, thinks about, and responds to her husband. Pray them for yourself.

> Love is patient, love is kind and is not jealous; love does not brag and is not arrogant, does not act unbecomingly; it does not seek its own, is not provoked, does not take into account a wrong suffered, does not rejoice in unrighteousness, but rejoices with the truth; bears all things, believes all things, hopes all things, endures all things. (1 Cor. 13:4–7)

Encourage the young women to love their husbands, to love their children, to be sensible, pure, workers at home, kind, being subject to their own husbands, so that the word of God will not be dishonored. (Titus 2:4–5)

Ↄ

You wives, be submissive to your own husbands so that even if any of them are disobedient to the word, they may be won without a word by the behavior of their wives, as they observe your chaste and respectful behavior. (1 Pet. 3:1–2)

Ↄ

Don't you wives realize that your husbands might be saved because of you? (1 Cor. 7:16 NLT)

Ↄ

The heart of her husband trusts in her, and he will not lack anything good. (Prov. 31:11 HCSB)

There are verses, particularly in Proverbs, that speak to the blessings of a man's integrity, his quest for wisdom, the leadership of his family, and God's desire to prosper him as he commits his many responsibilities to the Lord. Pray them for your husband.

Commit your works to the LORD,
And your plans will be established. (Prov. 16:3)

❦

When a man's ways are pleasing to the LORD,
He makes even his enemies to be at peace with
     him. (Prov. 16:7)

❦

Don't abandon wisdom, and she will watch over
     you;
love her, and she will guard you.
Wisdom is supreme—so get wisdom.
And whatever else you get, get understanding.
Cherish her, and she will exalt you;
if you embrace her, she will honor you.
     (Prov. 4:6–8 HCSB)

❦

Let your eyes look directly ahead
And let your gaze be fixed straight in front of you.
Watch the path of your feet,
And all your ways will be established.
     (Prov. 4:25–26)

❦

[Wisdom] will rescue you from a forbidden woman,
from a stranger with her flattering talk.
(Prov. 2:16 HCSB)

～

Don't fear sudden danger
or the ruin of the wicked when it comes,
for the LORD will be your confidence
and will keep your foot from a snare.
(Prov. 3:25–26 HCSB)

～

Trust in the LORD with all your heart,
And do not lean on your own understanding.
In all your ways acknowledge Him,
And He will make your paths straight. (Prov. 3:5–6)

There are other verses that lead a mother, a parent, to keep her children before the Lord and their protection in His hands. Pray them for your children.

In the fear of the LORD there is strong confidence,
And his children will have refuge. (Prov. 14:26)

～

Behold, I and the children whom the LORD has given me are for signs and wonders in Israel from the LORD of hosts. (Isa. 8:18)

❧

They were to rise and tell their children
so that they might put their confidence in God
and not forget God's works,
but keep His commands.
Then they would not be like their fathers,
a stubborn and rebellious generation,
a generation whose heart was not loyal
and whose spirit was not faithful to God.
    (Ps. 78:6–8 HCSB)

❧

I have no greater joy than this, to hear of my children walking in the truth. (3 John 4)

Then there are other passages that caution us not to fight with old weapons but to keep ourselves under control and trusting God's authority as we relate to one another:

Let no unwholesome word proceed from your mouth, but only such a word as is good for edification according to the need of the moment, so that it will give grace to those who hear. (Eph. 4:29)

Let your speech always be with grace, as though seasoned with salt, so that you will know how you should respond to each person. (Col. 4:6)

The end of all things is near; therefore, be of sound judgment and sober spirit for the purpose of prayer. Above all, keep fervent in your love for one another, because love covers a multitude of sins. Be hospitable to one another without complaint. (1 Pet. 4:7–9)

Pursue the things which make for peace and the building up of one another. (Rom. 14:19)

Not paying back evil for evil or insult for insult but, on the contrary, giving a blessing, since you were called for this, so that you can inherit a blessing. (1 Pet. 3:9 HCSB)

Homes and families, marriages and children can all too easily devolve into combat zones—which was the last thing in the world you ever foresaw when you pledged your life to your husband at the wedding altar, when you brought home that bundle of joy from the delivery room. What I'm telling you is this: You may not be able to control all the discord and unwise choices that occur in the various corners of your house or among the people you share a family with. But you can make sure the only place *you* engage in combat is in the heavenlies, in prayer, in secret. The enemy who's intent on disrupting the peace in your home doesn't flinch when you try to force your own fixes upon it, but he does start worrying when a wife, a mother, a daughter, or a sister starts avoiding the noise at the periphery and starts making some noise of her own, right outside the door to the devil's workshop.

I urge you, for the sake of your family, take the fight into your *prayer* room rather than your *living* room. Rip out one or two of those sheets in the back of this book, or grab your own stash of memo paper or sticky notes, and write down what you want to be sure your enemy hears you praying. Use the biblical promises and passages from this chapter as a framework to get started. Then take your vocal pleas to God instead of making your vocal presence such a common fixture around the house. Get ready to go to war for your family. And get ready to see some changes you've never seen happen before.

Your Past

Ending the Reign of Guilt, Shame, and Regret

If I were your enemy, I'd constantly remind you of your past mistakes and poor choices. I'd want to keep you burdened by shame and guilt, in hopes that you'll feel incapacitated by your many failings and see no point in even trying again. I'd work to convince you that you've had your chance and blown it—that your God may be able to forgive some people for some things, but not you . . . not for this.

It's awful. And it's personal.

A personal, unwelcome, unwarranted attack.

Using your forgiven past to poke holes in your future.

But that's exactly what the enemy does. He absolutely loves living in the past.

In *your* past. In *my* past.

And why not? Some of his best opportunities to sabotage our potential comes from there.

He carefully archives footage from our history so he can pull from those files and remind us what our days of defeat, sin, and failure looked like. You've seen them, same as I have, a million times. If your life is anything like mine, I'd imagine he's turned every room in the house into a screening room at one time or another, popping one of his old favorites into the player—for his amusement, for our humiliating shame and embarrassment.

It's a painful thing to watch. Even in reruns. *Especially* in reruns . . . because every time he cues it up again, it's with the fresh intent of mocking and maligning us, making us feel as unforgiven and unforgiveable as possible, and then even pointing the finger at all the other people who are more to blame, more at fault, than we should ever consider ourselves to be. If he can't make us feel judged, he'll try turning us into judges. So it's quite a show he puts on. And quite depressing. Mostly because, as he loves reminding us, we're the ones who've given him so much material to work with.

Under more constructive circumstances we might actually be able to *learn from it*—see another option we could've taken to avoid what ultimately happened, in order to not be so rash or gullible next time. We might be able to *teach from it*—help steer others who might one day face the same set of choices (our children, for example) toward an alternate ending that's likely to result in something more favorable for them. But in the hands of the enemy, it's always a horror film—*run from it, hide from it*—keep living and reliving it, over and over again. With no resolution, just a persistent dread and heartache. Never out of range from his cackling, accusing reappearance. Always at risk of having it jump up and scare us, just when we thought we and God had finally settled it for good.

And that's how, instead of living with assurance, we become bombarded with *shame*. Instead of celebrating God's grace, we feel undercut by continual *guilt* over the same old things. Instead of experiencing the ongoing, residual blessings of being regenerated by His Spirit—all things new—we're caught in the spin cycle of ceaseless *regrets*.

But prayer—fervent, strategic prayer—can change things. Even unchangeable things. Even things as unchangeable as real-life scenes from your past—what you did, what you didn't do, why you did it, why you didn't. No, prayer doesn't wipe them all away, doesn't pretend they never happened. And, no, it doesn't remove every natural, logical consequence from playing itself out. But just as God says to the ocean waves, "Thus far you shall come, but no farther" (Job 38:11), He has given us prayer to raise us up above the sea level of Satan's assaults from our past.

My past, for example, includes some unfortunate travels on US Highway 59 North, a major thoroughfare that runs through the heart of Houston, Texas. I did my undergraduate work in that city, and like a lot of college kids, I occasionally went down the wrong road when I should've stayed on the high road—which for me, all too personally, includes one particular exit off 59 North that sort of symbolizes some of the most regrettable choices I've made in my life. That road led to nowhere healthy. Nowhere beneficial. Nowhere I should've been in the first place. Perhaps you can relate. Choose from your own roads.

Many years later, long after college, events took me back to Houston for a summer speaking engagement. My hosts for the weekend picked me up at the airport, I climbed alone into the backseat, and they proceeded to drive me toward the hotel where I'd be staying—a route that diverted us for several miles onto that old familiar 59 North.

Being the kind, hospitable women they were, they continued to chat merrily as we sped past the various reflective signs on the highway. I'm not sure they even noticed how gradually quiet I was becoming in the back. But the mile marker numbers we were passing weren't just numbers to me; they were counting up to that one specific exit number that Satan was counting down in my mind with each condemning second. Flashbacks flooded. Tears began forming. I was fighting an old foe inside, and the spiritual battle was threatening to come spilling out all over.

And then . . . there it was. The exit ramp. The one I'd taken far too many times.

I couldn't breathe. My heart beat fast. My palms moistened with sweat.

And then, almost like a short whoosh of wind . . . the sign was gone. We were past it.

And at that precise moment, I sensed the voice of God speaking so clearly to me, saying: *Priscilla, wipe your tears away. That road is behind you now. I have other roads in store for you in the future, roads I've been preparing for you. Just as you've passed this exit of shame, so you now are beyond the pain that accompanied it. I make all things new.*

All things . . . new.

I turned clear around, looked out the rear windshield, and watched that exit sign fade into the distance.

Suddenly, the lilt of my new friends' voices bubbled back to the surface of my conscious hearing, and a fresh, rejuvenating smile strengthened my trembling lower lip. I looked ahead and, for the first time in my life, I saw what Houston looked like beyond that exit on 59 North, a stretch of road I'd never traveled before. And I saw a side of God's grace that I'd never, ever experienced. The past was in the past. It didn't have permission to touch me anymore. And just like on the freeway, I would soon be traveling to new places of freedom and fullness I'd never seen before.

It was done. I was free.

The enemy's bad-girl accusations against us come with a statute of limitations. He can rant and threaten and how-dare-you all he wants, but here's why you can plug your ears, ignore his accusations, and sing God's praise while you walk away with real pardon in your heart.

First, God doesn't live in the past. Because God—your God—exists outside of time. To Him, the past that so haunts and hamstrings you, the past that so ruffles and frustrates you, is not in the past at all. In prayer, you are alone with a God who sees you only as you *are* and have always *been* since that beautiful moment when you placed faith in Him—holy, righteous, and blameless; past, present, and future. He forgives your guilt, removes your shame, and declares His work an established, all-the-time fact. Prayer does a complete end run around Satan's pitiful accusations, ushering us into an eternal realm with God where "the past" doesn't even compute.

And second, we only live by grace anyway. All that stuff Satan tries hanging over our head—those forgiven failings of ours are no longer reasons for shame but are now monuments to the totally amazing grace of God. I mean, just *look* at what He is able to forgive. Even this. Even that. *Yes, devil, even THAT! Isn't God incredible? That He could forgive even that?!*

The glory our God receives, and will eternally receive, from having saved our souls doesn't come from all the good things we do for Him. His glory comes from creating people of purity and spiritual passion who once did things like *that*. Like *we've* done. Like *you've* done. Like *I've* done.

So talk it up, devil. Because as high as you choose to ratchet it up, you're only showing off "the breadth and length and height and depth" (Eph. 3:18) of the love of Christ extended toward me!

Satan can be the "accuser of [the] brethren" all he wants to be (Rev. 12:10), but he can't change what the cross has done to throw all his accusations out of court—every last one of them—on an undeniably divine technicality.

Again, one of the qualities that makes the gospel so real and so great is that it doesn't eliminate our past but just so thoroughly deals with it. God forgives it. He changes it. He transforms all that mess into this huge mountain of grace that only takes us higher and closer to Him. So now, instead of being a reason for endless shame, guilt, and regret, our past is a reason for endless worship and free-flowing testimony.

And for continual, grateful, heartfelt prayer.

CALL TO PRAYER

I realize, when I bring up the subject of the past, I have no real idea what populates that period of time for you. I hope you've seen, as I've talked about the height and depth of God's love and grace (a phrase that comes from Ephesians 3:16–19) that I'm not minimizing what's back there—the extent of what you've done or what's been done to you. But the devil wants you to think that your past is worse than everybody else's. Or he wants to suggest to you that, given your religious background and what you profess to be in public, your past sins (though perhaps not the shocking, scandalous type) still disqualify you from parading around all Christian-like.

Look, here's the truth: There's not one of us—not one— who can't stare back into our past and wish a hundred times we'd done a hundred things differently. And the reason it's only a hundred today is probably just because our memory isn't what it used to be. Not to mention, despite our best efforts, we keep feeding our enemy new clips of failure to choose from and compile. And as soon as they fade into the past, he fires up the projector and invites himself over for popcorn, to make sure we're seeing how bad it is and how bad we are.

Yes, we're all on a journey here. We're not perfect. We all struggle. We can tell from the fatigue we feel and the stiffness in our spiritual joints that we haven't always taken good care of ourselves. But prayer wakes us up with mercies from God that are "new every morning" (Lam. 3:23). Prayer is how we start to stretch and feel limber again, feel loose, ready to take on the world. And when we start applying prayer to particular muscle groups—like our confidence in Christ and His victory over our past—our whole body and our whole being start to percolate with fresh energy, with the blood-pumping results of applied faith.

So as you begin crafting a strategy for crushing Satan's backdoor assault on your daily freedom and joy, think back again to that helpful guide we've been using:

- *Praise:* Thank Him for completely forgiving you, cleansing you, changing you.
- *Repentance:* See the foolishness of anything that perpetuates old sin patterns, and by His Spirit walk away.
- *Asking:* Ask for freedom, for release, for the ability to deflect lies and embrace truth.
- *Yes:* Because you, by His resurrection power, can now walk in a new way of life.

Therefore if anyone is in Christ, he is a new creature; the old things passed away; behold, new things have come. (2 Cor. 5:17)

∽

Once you were dead because of your disobedience and your many sins. You used to live in sin, just like the rest of the world, obeying the devil—the commander of the powers in the unseen world. He is the spirit at work in the hearts of those who refuse to obey God. All of us used to live that way, following the passionate desires and inclinations of our sinful nature. By our very nature we were subject to God's anger, just like everyone else. But God is so rich in mercy, and he loved us so much, that even though we were dead because of our sins, he gave us life when he raised Christ from the dead. (It is only by God's grace that you have been saved!) (Eph. 2:1–5 NLT)

༄

Thus says the LORD . . .
Do not call to mind the former things,
Or ponder things of the past.
Behold, I will do something new,
Now it will spring forth;
Will you not be aware of it?
I will even make a roadway in the wilderness,
Rivers in the desert. (Isa. 43:16, 18–19)

༄

Sing praise to the LORD, you His godly ones,
And give thanks to His holy name.
For His anger is but for a moment,
His favor is for a lifetime;
Weeping may last for the night,
But a shout of joy comes in the morning.
    (Ps. 30:4–5)

❧

He gives strength to the weary,
And to him who lacks might He increases power.
Though youths grow weary and tired,
And vigorous young men stumble badly,
Yet those who wait for the LORD
Will gain new strength;
They will mount up with wings like eagles,
They will run and not get tired,
They will walk and not become weary.
    (Isa. 40:29–31)

❧

He has said to me, "My grace is sufficient for you, for power is perfected in weakness." Most gladly, therefore, I will rather boast about my weaknesses, so that the power of Christ may dwell in me. (2 Cor. 12:9)

❧

Jesus Christ is the same yesterday and today and forever. (Heb. 13:8)

The past, for all its attempts at confining and condemning us, possesses limits that our enemy doesn't want us to know about. Well, now we do. And so here we go. We're moving on. And he can just sit back there in the dark and watch all those home movies of his, all by himself. Because our real life in Christ is just a lot more exciting.

Here's to freedom . . . yours and mine.

In Jesus' name.

Amen.

YOUR FEARS

CONFRONTING YOUR WORRIES, CLAIMING YOUR CALLING

If I were your enemy, I'd magnify your fears, making them appear insurmountable, intimidating you with enough worries until avoiding them becomes your driving motivation. I would use anxiety to cripple you, to paralyze you, leaving you indecisive, clinging to safety and sameness, always on the defensive because of what might happen. When you hear the word faith, all I'd want you to hear is "unnecessary risk."

A fun road trip to Austin, Texas.

Just me, my big sister Chrystal, and one of our closest friends, Shawna.

Chrystal was driving, I was in the front passenger seat, and Shawna was in the back . . . talking about something she'd been thinking about doing but why she couldn't do it and how she felt bad about not doing it but why it didn't matter because she could never do it anyway. On and on like that. Chrystal and I looked ahead out the windshield, sipping our lattes and listening, nodding in sympathy and genuine concern. When we tried to press her on what her real hesitations were, she kept talking and rationalizing and deflecting and defending until she finally nearly snapped our heads back with a really unexpected, highly exasperated, *"Because I'm not READY!"*

[road noise, the low hum of air coming from the A/C vents]

"Because I'm SCARED!"

Allow me to step back for a second and do a better job of introducing Shawna to you. Because if all you knew about her was what I'd just described, I'd be giving you the completely wrong impression. My friend is a devoted wife of nearly twenty years and a highly accomplished, highly intelligent mother of three. Tremendously adept at managing a full household. Dynamic, outspoken believer. Trains hard-core for marathons. (I don't even know how many of those things she's run.) She's full of energy but with tenderness too, as well as a knack for giving people spot-on insights about their deepest needs and toughest questions. As a licensed counselor who runs her own business, she's the kind who gets sent referrals when people hit a dead-end through all other routes of care and treatment and simply aren't going to make it unless they see someone of Shawna's caliber. She's the best in her field . . . and in every other way too.

In the months leading up to our outing, however, the Lord had been fairly obvious and direct in leading her to start cutting back on her caseload and start focusing on doing some writing—cataloging all this stellar wisdom she's been dishing out for all these years and collecting it into resources that can multiply her ministry of counsel and encouragement to who knows how many others. Her husband had told her, "Honey, just do it. We'll be all right financially. I believe in you and in what you can do, and I truly want you following the Lord on this. We'll do what we need to do to make it happen. I'm totally behind you." So everything was lining up. Every indication on her spiritual radar was tracking with this new direction.

Only one problem: she was scared.

Master's degree. Business owner. College teacher.

Even a woman like her can get scared.

And now, in the car on the way back from a weekend with friends, tears rolled down her cheeks as she chronicled her internal struggle: What if I can't do it? What if I make all these arrangements, release my client list, sit down in front of that computer, and nothing comes out? Nothing makes sense? Worse yet, what if I do get some stuff written,

start to feel pretty good about it, but nobody likes it? Or
what if they're too nice to say they don't like it, but I can tell
from what they *do* say (and *don't* say) that I've failed miser-
ably? What if no avenues crop up where I can get my work
published or distributed? Even if I can, what if people don't
find it helpful or useful or any different from anything else
they've read? What if the financial adjustment we'll need to
make in order for me to do it means my kids will have to
give up some of the activities they love? What if it all ends
up being a total waste of time and energy? What if it's all
just some sort of ego trip or head game, something I'm pro-
jecting onto myself?

"*I'm not ready, y'all—I'm SCARED!*"

She sniffled. Wiped away a few runaway tears.

I wanted to console her—reach back and rub her
knee—to say, *there, there, I understand.* But in that moment,
other words started coming out instead before I'd really pro-
cessed what they might sound like, spoken with a fierceness
and intensity that shocked even me.

"*Do it anyway!*" I said, spinning around almost a full
turn from my front-seat position, looking directly into her
face. "Shawna, if the *only* reason you aren't moving forward
is fear, then don't you see that the enemy is trying to paralyze you? He's the one behind this. Don't sit there and let
him do that. Don't let him stop you from moving forward. I
don't care *how* afraid or not ready you may feel. Obey God
anyway!"

She stared at me blankly. I stared back. Both of us stunned by my indignation.

The fact is, I was mad. Still am. Mad at the enemy for messing with my friend like that. And I'm mad at him for messing with you too . . . and with me. With all of us. Anytime I begin seeing that the only thing keeping me from receiving everything God wants to give me is the fear tactic the enemy is using against me—*it makes me mad.* I start feeling a holy indignation rolling up over my shoulders and picking me up from behind. Because if he's working *that* hard to keep me from moving forward, there must be some blessing or beauty from heaven he's trying to divert me from. And I'm just not having it, not anymore, not from *him.* I hope you're not either.

The fact is this: fear is one of Satan's primary schemes for crippling God's people. I'm not talking about legitimate concern. I'm not talking about the protective warnings of wisdom and godly counsel. I'm talking about *fear.* Incessant worry. Up-all-night anxiety. Worst-case scenarios becoming the only probabilities you can think about. Fears like these, instead of simply raising our blood pressure, ought to set off some fire alarms. *Why am I feeling so paralyzed like this?*

We clearly know from Scripture that "God has not given us a spirit of fear, but of power and of love and of a sound mind" (2 Tim. 1:7 NKJV). So whenever you sense a "spirit of fear" invading any particular area of your life, you can know by process of elimination that it's not coming from God . . .

which only leaves one other spiritual place it could be originating from . . . which ought to make you wonder why it's
there. Aren't you at least a little bit curious what he's trying
to keep you from experiencing?

I'm pretty sure you're familiar with the story of Moses
and the children of Israel, pinned up against the waters of
the Red Sea while the Egyptian pharaoh and his armies
were bearing down hard from behind. Israel was fast in the
process of being surrounded by people whose nation had
brutalized them and their ancestors for four long, horrendous
centuries. No escape. And the only direction that wasn't
swarming with enemy hordes, the one path God was directing His people to go, lay straight ahead through the sea.

So these two million Hebrews had every reason to be
terrified. Mortified really. There was no swimming out of
this one.

And yet, in the face of such impossible circumstances,
with the odds so heavily stacked against them, and with no
indicator of the miracle that God had planned, Moses said
to the people, "Do not fear!" (Exod. 14:13). His very first
instruction to them was *not to be afraid*.

Notice that Moses wasn't telling them not to *feel* fear.
The prospect of looming death will just kind of do that. On
its own. Fear is a natural human response to a lot of things,
a Red Sea moment being one of them. So he knew they
would *feel* fear, but he was telling them not to *wallow* in it.
Not to choose it. Not make friends with it. Not entertain

it, engage it. Because if they did, they risked not sticking around long enough to experience the stunning miracle their God was about to perform. And even more, they risked not getting to the other side. To the Promised Land. To the milk and to the honey. To destiny.

Oh, so *that's* what the enemy wanted fear to keep them from obtaining. *That's* what they'd all be singing about in the next chapter, while Pharaoh's army was being swallowed whole by the waters and Israel was now just a hop and a skip from Sinai.

And *that's* what he hopes fear will keep you from obtaining too.

Your destiny.

Let me say this: I do know firsthand how the despair of intimidation feels when it's strangling you around the neck. I know the kind of paralysis that can harden around you when you're scared to death about going through with something you've committed to do, and you just don't think you've got what it takes to do it. I've known those times—like you perhaps—when all we feel like doing is pulling the drapes, climbing back under the covers, and wishing the next few hours (or days? or weeks?) would please just go away.

But whether you need a gentle hand today reaching out to hold yours, or if (like my sweet friend Shawna) you could use a little tough love right now to shake yourself awake from the stupor of all those excuses, the prescription is still the same . . .

Do. Not. Be. Afraid.

This issue of fear is so well-known and important to God that more than three hundred times in Scripture He tells His people—in one form or another—not to be afraid. "Fear not." "Be ye not afraid." "Do not fear." Look it up. It's everywhere. You know those times when you're searching high and low for just one verse to tell you what God wants you to do? Well, here's three hundred of them. And they're all saying the same thing: "Don't be afraid."

It's the enemy telling you, "Be *very* afraid."

Is that the kind of junk he's been feeding you lately? Twenty million reasons why you can't? Can't kick the habit? Can't stand up and lead a Bible study? Can't help start that inner-city ministry? Not qualified enough for that job? Can't do *this*, could *never* do that, be crazy to even *think* about doing that *other* thing?

Why not? Might take too much time? Not to mention the pressure? The germs? Do I really want to risk the rejection of being told no? Don't I realize what I'd be giving up in terms of security and salary and insurance benefits? What would people think if I did something so audacious, something out of my normal routine and pattern? Wouldn't I just be opening myself up to criticism and catty comments? What about my food allergies, my fear of flying, all my other various intolerances?

Are those the kind of speed bumps and roadblocks he's been laying in front of you, seemingly all your life?

He's just full of it. Full of excuses. Invested in cramming you full of fear. Why? Because fear is the antithesis of faith. And faith is what allows you to step foot on the soil of your destiny.

Hear me out, and hear me good. I'm about to write a long, run-on sentence, but I want you hanging on every word: If God has given you clear direction, like He gave the children of Israel (or like He's given to my friend Shawna)— direction that's confirmed by His written Word and by the sounding board of wise, godly counsel—and your only real reason for resisting Him is because you're *afraid* of what following Him down this path might mean or cost or entail, then you're not only on the threshold of being disobedient, you're about to miss an opportunity to give God some fresh, new glory by doing what He's wanting to do through you, which is the true impetus behind His invitation for you to join Him on this scary adventure in the first place.

In fervent prayer, we discover something: Our God is fearless. And because *He* is fearless, we can be fearless too. When His presence is with us and going before us, no Red Sea should faze us or give us pause.

So despite your hesitation, say yes.

Walk on. Have faith. Fear not.

CALL TO PRAYER

God wouldn't tell us not to be afraid—or tell it to us so often—if He didn't fully realize that fear, worry, anxiety, queasiness, cold feet, sweaty palms, dry mouth, and racing heartbeats are our first, natural reaction to some of the challenges of following Him, especially those (like most) that don't come with clear, step-by-step instructions on how to handle every possible hiccup or contingency.

The enemy, of course—aware of this—is always lurking nearby, eager to animate and agitate those concerns of ours so they keep us up at night and interfere with our ability to think clearly. He even goes a step further, stamping a spirit of fear on the very things He knows are God's best options for us. But God is always there as well—far outranking him in strength—to hear our troubled prayers, reaffirm His fearless promises, and deliver the next bit of lamplight we need for walking steadily in His direction.

Prayer is the difference maker. An invitation for honesty, yes, for telling him how you feel—infused with the assurance and fearless confidence that comes from God's promises.

Remember these worries of yours? They're not just stray thoughts; they're deliberate strategies. Strategies to derail you from your destiny and calling. And the way to fight them is with a deliberate prayer strategy of your own.

When I am afraid,

I will put my trust in You.

In God, whose word I praise,

In God I have put my trust;

I shall not be afraid.

What can mere man do to me? (Ps. 56:3–4)

❧

For God has not given us a spirit of fear, but of power and of love and of a sound mind. (2 Tim. 1:7 NKJV)

❧

The word of the LORD came to me:

I chose you before I formed you in the womb;

I set you apart before you were born.

I appointed you a prophet to the nations.

But I protested, "Oh no, Lord, GOD! Look, I don't

know how to speak since I am only a youth."

Then the LORD said to me:

Do not say, "I am only a youth,"

for you will go to everyone I send you to

and speak whatever I tell you.

Do not be afraid of anyone,

for I will be with you to deliver you.

(Jer. 1:4–8 HCSB)

❧

Peace I leave with you; My peace I give to you; not as the world gives do I give to you. Do not let your heart be troubled, nor let it be fearful. (John 14:27)

❧

"For I know the plans that I have for you," declares the LORD, "plans for welfare and not for calamity to give you a future and a hope." (Jer. 29:11)

❧

I will instruct you and teach you in the way which
    you should go;
I will counsel you with My eye upon you.
    (Ps. 32:8)

❧

I will give you the right words and such wisdom that none of your opponents will be able to reply or refute you! (Luke 21:15 NLT)

❧

My sheep hear My voice, and I know them, and they follow Me; and I give eternal life to them, and they will never perish; and no one will snatch them out of My hand. My Father, who has given them to Me, is greater than all; and no one is able to snatch them out of the Father's hand. (John 10:27–29)

⌒

Therefore, brethren, since we have confidence to enter the holy place by the blood of Jesus, by a new and living way which He inaugurated for us . . . let us hold fast the confession of our hope without wavering, for He who promised is faithful. (Heb. 10:19–20, 23)

As you take these Scriptures and get ready to craft your prayer, I thought you'd want to know that Shawna—she's doing it. Instead of letting fear be the loudest voice in the room, she's been able to go back and implement obedience, going forward as instructed. She's not the one crying in the backseat anymore. She's thrown *fear* into the backseat. And good for her . . . because *nobody's* telling my Holy Spirit fuel-injected friend that she's not good enough, not ready, not capable . . . that she *can't*.

Oh, yes, she *can*.

And so can you.

YOUR PURITY

STAYING STRONG IN YOUR MOST SUSCEPTIBLE PLACES

If I were your enemy, I'd tempt you toward certain sins, making you believe they are basically (even biologically) unavoidable. I'd study your tendencies and proclivities till I learned the precise conditions that make you the most likely to indulge them. And then I'd strike right there. Again and again. Wear you down. Because if I can't separate you from God forever, I can at least set you at odds with Him for the time being.

"Don't touch that! You don't know where it's been!"

I've said it to my three sons time and time again. Wonder how many other little kids have heard their parents say something similar, usually while lunging across the playground or the sandbox, horrified at their son's or daughter's unsanitary sense of curiosity.

I know I'm not your mama. But I do think of you as a friend. And when it comes to the enemy's specific, strategic, most enticing temptations against you and against your purity, I hope you'll imagine me as a blur coming up fast in your peripheral vision, calling out to you with an urgent voice, both arms waving wildly, "DON'T! TOUCH! THAT!"

. . . because both of us know *exactly* where's it's been.

That enticing temptation that tickles your curiosity, piques your interest, and placates your personal proclivities has been festering in the devil's sick, sinister mind all morning, all week, all year maybe. Just sitting there, soaking up vileness and filth. Cruelty and conspiracy. Waiting for the right time—the moment when you are most weakened and susceptible to attack. But once he's cleaned it up for presentation, sliding it meticulously into view, you'd think it was the shiniest, most desirable bit of unclaimed satisfaction you've ever seen. He sets it out there where your eyes can't help but be drawn toward it—at least, you know, to pick it up and look at it. Feel it. Play with it.

The moral compromise. The unhealthy habit. The enticing addiction. The allure toward sexual impurity. Do

you think their uncanny ability to show up when you happen to be exhausted or hungry or lonely is just coincidence?
Don't you detect some design at work in the timing, the
placement, the package?

Look at what we know from Satan's temptation of Christ
in Matthew 4. The devil came out into the wilderness where
Jesus had been fasting for forty days, a time when (physically
speaking) the Lord was hungry, alone, tired, depleted. What
better setup and situation to make the suggestion of, well . . .
bread? I mean, I don't know about you, but slide a warm roll
in my direction, topped with a smear of soft butter, and I'm
a goner. Even when I'm *not* hungry. But that's the enemy's
way. Precision, personalization, and persistence. He's always
scouting for what Luke's Gospel describes as the "opportune
time" (4:13)—the moment when a well-placed temptation is
most likely to be its most irresistible.

So again I ask—the devil's temptations, the ones
he picks out and personalizes for you . . . coincidence?
Uncalculated? Just happenstance?

Stop and see what's happening. Stop at the place where
you first recognize the scent of temptation in the air. And
before you touch it, remember . . . *remember where it's been.*
Remember where it came from and who's behind it. And
if it's one of those repeat temptations you've been battling
against for years, remember the places it's taken you . . . the
places it *always* ends up taking you. Because as soon as you
say yes to it, you're headed there again.

And you know it.

The kind of prayer strategy we're about to employ treats every temptation as the potent, life-threatening stick of dynamite that it is. Despite how inviting it seems, despite how natural it feels, despite how much simpler the rest of your day would seem to go if you just gave in and went along with it, temptations are never innocuous. The consequences are never minimal. The waves of your choice will ripple outward into your heart, mind, soul, and body, possibly even to future generations.

Sin has consequences. Always has and always will. Keep this revelation fixed squarely in your mind. Because whether we like it or not, here's how the spiritual economy of life works for believers: Obedience to God garners intimacy and nearness, divine blessing and favor. Always. And disobedience creates a sense of distance and loss, grief and regret. Always. Sometimes the consequences of caving to temptation are practical and tangible, changing your daily experience, drastically enough in certain cases to fundamentally affect the rest of your life. But no matter how immediately noticeable the cost, the ripple effects of sin always affect your connection with the Father. And this, *this,* is exactly what the enemy is hoping for. It's why he is so personalized and meticulous in his advances to tempt you.

Impurity weakens your praying—which in turn weakens your power. When our lives are not aligned with the teaching of Scripture and the transforming work of God's

Spirit—when we're resisting His wise, loving instruction concerning our lifestyle and attitudes—our prayer closets start to feel like soundproof rooms. Our spiritual armor becomes little more than the plastic, painted stuff they sell as a kit in the toy section of the Christian bookstore. The energy we expect our prayers to access and generate is momentarily choked off and shorted out. We've compromised the system. We've created a bottleneck. We're leaking oil, leaking power. We end up, in practical terms, living like the double-minded man in the New Testament book of James, who the Bible says "should not expect to receive anything from the Lord" because he's "unstable in all his ways" (James 1:7–8 HCSB).

One of the psalm writers painfully summarized it this way: "If I regard wickedness in my heart, the Lord will not hear" (Ps. 66:18). It's not because God's hand is "so short that it cannot save; nor is His ear so dull that it cannot hear. But your iniquities have made a separation between you and your God, and your sins have hidden His face from you so that He does not hear" (Isa. 59:1–2). Separation. That's what sin creates. Which is why the enemy is dead set on crafting temptations for our lives. He knows that the "effectual fervent prayer" that James 5:16 (KJV) says "availeth much" contains parameters. Prayers that have power come from a person in pursuit of righteous living.

Yes, righteousness matters.

That's why you and I must deliberately strategize in prayer for the daily, ongoing protection of our purity. Prayer keeps us on guard, our spiritual radar sensitive to the enemy's ploys and clever decoys. Without this close contact with the Father, we become convinced that our careless behavior, our decisions, our habits, our general sense of what qualifies as worthwhile entertainment is somehow OK, that it's "not so bad." Yet all the while the enemy's carefully crafted options of impurity chip away at our spiritual reserves and effectiveness.

The devil's strategy is to make us believe impurity is, well . . . normal . . . that nobody's hurt if we keep a few forbidden things on hand and enjoy them from time to time. No big deal. But if we were steadily engaged in fervent prayer—with *our* strategy counteracting *his* strategy—we'd see in a snap that unrighteousness is not "no big deal." It's a house of horrors. It is a *totally* upside-down way to live.

Speaking of things that are upside-down . . .

When my boys and I go fishing, we like to walk over to a small pond not far from our house on a friend's property. And fairly often when we go there, if we've got the time, we'll decide not just to fish from the bank but to use the small boat that's always sitting nearby . . . always flipped over on its top, the bottom of the hull pointing upward.

The reason the owners leave it upended like that is so the water it collects during even a short swim in the pond will drain out afterward and not rust the metal. But every time one of the boys suggests we drag the boat in, we're extremely careful (or at least *I* am) when turning it over from its resting place on the grass, in case any wildlife has wandered underneath and made itself at home. Frogs, lizards, turtles, snakes. We've seen them all. The damp, cool, shady environment beneath the overturned rowboat is a perfect place for bad company to come hang out.

Now listen, these critters don't need a personal invitation to come be a part of our day. No need for that. Leaving that boat upside-down creates the right environment, and *that* is invitation enough.

The same thing is equally true for our lives. Impure living, impure thinking, impure relationships, impure affections—upside-down living—creates the perfect environment and breeding ground for demonic activity. It invites him in and then fosters the perfect place for his turmoil and trouble to thrive. Unrighteousness disrupts our peace. It scares away any lasting sense of rest and contentment. It spoils what could otherwise be enjoyable. It complicates experiences that were meant to be nothing but pleasures and blessings. We can't knowingly create this kind of an environment—the kind that invites the devil to make himself at home—and then blame God for whatever sense of distance we may feel from Him. We must choose righteous, right-side-up living, while committing to pray fervently and consistently that we'll recognize the ploys of the enemy the moment they come into view.

Because not only does our *prayer* deflect the enemy, but our *purity* deflects the enemy.

God calls you to purity because He wants your heart protected and at rest, inhospitable to the devil and his intentions. God wants you full of power and confidence and spiritual vitality. He wants you free to bless and encourage others, to receive and celebrate His goodness, to become such a stick-of-dynamite prayer warrior that Satan just hates hearing your coffeepot heat up in the morning.

How'd you like to start experiencing *those* kinds of consequences? Not the ones that leave you feeling disgusted and despondent, miserable from another failure, but totally energized instead. In Jesus.

This doesn't mean you'll never do anything wrong again. We're not built for that. Not yet anyway. Vestiges of sin still hide in the nooks and crannies of our flesh, and they're magnetically drawn toward the allure of temptation. Even the apostle Paul admitted to the struggle. "I do not understand," he said. "I am doing the very thing I hate" (Rom. 7:15). "I have the desire to do what is right, but not the ability to carry it out" (v. 18 ESV). Boy, do I hear you.

But a prayer strategy can even help you here too . . . because the only thing worse than not prevailing in purity at any given moment is failing to respond humbly to God's discipline after a setback. His conviction is never meant to berate you but simply to correct you and bring you back to Himself. No divide. No separation. *Pure.*

Purity leads us to fervent prayer, and fervent prayer leads us to purity. And when we start putting this cycle to work, building momentum like a spiritual turbine, surrounding our hearts with the nearness of God's protection, we strip Satan of the power to rope us down to the same old cycle of sin we've always known.

We say to him, in so many words . . .

Can't touch this.

CALL TO PRAYER

God is inviting you right now to realms of glory. To wide-open spaces of genuine freedom and possibility. To scenes where victory can become, no kidding, an everyday occurrence. You'll think you're just sitting in whatever little place you call your prayer closet, but you'll actually be in a whole new world where He is King and where even your nastiest individual sins are utterly subject to His power.

Now *here's* the place you want to be.

The kind of place a girl like you and me could really settle down and be at home.

So grab a pencil, get comfortable, and write them down. Your struggles, I mean. Name them specifically, individually. Call them out from hiding. Unmask them and make them show their faces. Because when you come to these Scriptures I've printed out, you're going to find some phrases of truth in there that, while you probably *know* them, perhaps you haven't been *praying* them in connection with specific areas of temptation in your life—Scriptures that authorize you to throw off the chains of slavery to sin and put on the breastplate of righteousness. Find the phrases that speak to your heart most clearly in connection with the specific issues you're struggling with, and then use them (along with all kinds of other Bible verses the Spirit will give you) as part of your customized prayer strategy.

Don't worry now. This job of overcoming temptation and living in purity is not something you're tasked with pulling off on your own. When God saved you, it was with the understanding that He'd be providing you "sanctification by the Spirit" all along the way (2 Thess. 2:13), from the inside out, His purity and holiness changing your heart until it comes through as purity and holiness in action. As you yield yourself to Him in prayer, inviting Him to do His work, it won't just be the sweaty, exhausting chore of avoiding sin. It'll be God Himself building up strength at your core, enabling you by His resurrection power to passionately pursue righteousness. Then go from your prayer closet, ready to "walk in a manner worthy of the calling with which you have been called" (Eph. 4:1). Strategize your obedience as diligently as the enemy is strategizing those temptations.

You'll be blown away with the blessings of purity. So why not make them the norm rather than the exception?

And here's why they *can* be . . .

There is now no condemnation for those who are in Christ Jesus. For the law of the Spirit of life in Christ Jesus has set you free from the law of sin and of death. (Rom. 8:1–2)

◠

He Himself bore our sins in His body on the cross, so that we might die to sin and live to righteousness; for by His wounds you were healed. For you were continually straying like sheep, but now you have returned to the Shepherd and Guardian of your souls. (1 Pet. 2:24–25)

◠

Therefore do not let sin reign in your mortal body so that you obey its lusts, and do not go on presenting the members of your body to sin as instruments of unrighteousness; but present yourselves to God as those alive from the dead, and your members as instruments of righteousness to God. For sin shall not be master over you, for you are not under law but under grace. (Rom. 6:12–14)

◠

Walk by the Spirit, and you will not carry out the desire of the flesh. (Gal. 5:16)

❧

What fruit was produced then from the things you are now ashamed of? For the end of those things is death. But now, since you have been liberated from sin and have become enslaved to God, you have your fruit, which results in sanctification—and the end is eternal life! For the wages of sin is death, but the gift of God is eternal life in Christ Jesus our Lord. (Rom. 6:21–23 HCSB).

❧

No temptation has overtaken you but such as is common to man; and God is faithful, who will not allow you to be tempted beyond what you are able, but with the temptation will provide the way of escape also, so that you will be able to endure it. (1 Cor. 10:13)

❧

Stand firm therefore, having girded your loins with truth, and having put on the breastplate of righteousness. (Eph. 6:14)

❧

Satan has demanded permission to sift you like wheat; but I have prayed for you, that your faith may not fail. (Luke 22:31–32)

꙳

My flesh and my heart may fail,
But God is the strength of my heart, my portion
    forever. (Ps. 73:26)

꙳

The Lord knows how to rescue the godly from temptation. (2 Pet. 2:9)

Let me just give you one more. Psalm 91 says that God has created a shelter for you, a place where the covering shadow of His love thoroughly shades you from the high-noon heat of temptation. Your God, it says, is a refuge. Your God is a fortress. Your God is trustworthy. And your God is a deliverer. The arrows can fly by day, pestilence can stalk in the darkness, destruction can lie in wait for you right in the middle of the afternoon. "A thousand may fall at your side and ten thousand at your right hand, but it shall not approach you. . . . For you have made the LORD, my refuge, even the Most High, your dwelling place" (Ps. 91:7, 9).

And then . . . you are safe.

YOUR PRESSURES

RECLAIMING PEACE, REST, AND CONTENTMENT

If I were your enemy, I'd make everything seem urgent, as if it's all yours to handle. I'd bog down your calendar with so many expectations you couldn't tell the difference between what's important and what's not. Going and doing, guilty for ever saying no, trying to control it all, but just being controlled by it all instead. . . . If I could keep you busy enough, you'd be too overwhelmed to even realize how much work you're actually saving me.

Pressure.

Pressure to keep up. Pressure to keep going. Pressure to stay ahead, stay afloat, stay relevant. Pressure to do for others what they maybe ought to be doing for themselves.

Pressure to plan for your retirement years. Pressure to lose weight and stay young looking. Pressure to take on another ministry project at church. Pressure to always be the one they can count on to say yes. Pressure to jam another activity for your kids into the schedule. Pressure to do a better job of keeping a journal, organizing your pantry and closets, getting your Christmas shopping done early . . . then posting your clever thoughts and carefully posed pictures on Instagram when you're finished.

Pressure to perform a certain way, look a certain way, dress a certain way, be interested in certain things. To be the perfect parent, the perfect wife, the perfect daughter, the perfect friend, the perfect employee, the perfect party planner, the perfect image of everything that everybody else expects you to be.

Oh, and the pressure not to be the first one who cracks.

Under the *pressure*.

Granted, there's a baseline level of pressure that's necessary to keep us from settling into laziness and self-absorption. Life without *any* pressure wouldn't be what's best for us. But life with *this* much pressure? From a nonstop pace? A schedule that never allows time for rest or refreshment or maybe actually *enjoying* the people we're staying so busy with? Pressure from the unrealistic demands we place on ourselves through our perfectionism, obsession, control, the making of appearances? Pressure from the unreasonable demands that *others* place on us? Pressure that makes us feel like we might be wrong . . . or selfish . . . or coldhearted . . . or snooty to enforce margin and boundaries in our schedule so that we can actually maintain enough time to be obedient to what the Lord has called us to do?

I've noticed a few common threads running through pressures like these. And each of them leads back to a common source . . . leads back to someone who (as usual) is seeking to rob you of the most common ingredients to a fruitful life—a life of truly eternal significance—the life you were created by God to live.

First, consider this. Ever notice how many of the pressures in your life resemble *slavery*? Like you're just being bossed around, day in and day out? "Do this . . . go there . . . now come back over here . . . do it again . . ." Slaves don't rest. Slaves just work. They don't control their agenda for the day; the day's agenda controls *them*. That's the regular dynamic they've come to expect; it's what others expect of them as well.

The enemy's intention is always to enslave you. Primarily, of course, his stock-in-trade is keeping you bound up and bogged down by all the sins Christ has already died to set you free from. But when that doesn't work, when you defeat him on the normal temptation front, he's not out of other ideas . . . because he's actually not biased toward limiting his temptations to *bad* things. He can enslave you to *good* things too. Your job, your ministry, even your recreational hobbies—nothing is so healthy and life-giving that he can't turn it into a cruel taskmaster, one that bosses you around and runs your life.

When God delivered the ancient Israelites from four hundred years of bondage in Egypt, slavery was all they'd ever known (Exod. 1:8–14). All night, all day, all work, no play. The rhythms and demands of slavery had been internalized within them from birth. Whatever their taskmasters said, that's what they did. Refusing wasn't a choice. Saying no wasn't an option. I'm sure they didn't like it, but what could they do about it?—till the Lord sent Moses and ten mighty plagues and delivered them from the iron clutches of Pharaoh.

Israel was free. They were no longer a slave people.

But being officially declared free doesn't automatically take the slave mentality out of a person's heart and mind, now, does it? God knew He would need to radically adjust their perspectives in order to get them thinking like people who weren't slaves anymore.

Enter . . . the Sabbath.

Think for a second how the introduction of Sabbath among the Ten Commandments must have struck the people who first heard it announced: "Six days you shall labor and do all your work, but the seventh day is a sabbath

of the LORD your God; in it *you shall not do any work"* (Exod.
20:9–10, author emphasis).

Don't. Work?

These people had never heard these words before.
Never been given that alternative. The whole idea behind
this Hebrew word *shabbat*—"to cease, to stop, to pause"—
was a totally foreign concept. All their background and
training were built around going, not stopping. Working, not
resting. Complying, not declining or decompressing.

So you'd think the prospect of being allowed (no, *told*)
to take regular breaks from their weekly work would sound
incredible, relieving, reprieving. Right? Think again. They
balked against their seventh-day vacation allotment and
went out to work anyway (Exod. 16:27–30).

Why does this concept of stopping, resting, shutting
off, stepping away, pulling back, taking a deep breath—the
biblical *command* of Sabbath—why was it so hard for them?

Same reason it's so hard for us.

Because to some degree, we're slaves just as they were.

The thought of deliberately choosing a rhythm of rest
and margin around our full slate of activities feels almost
unthinkable—because it lands on people who still think the
way a slave thinks. People who've been trained through the
years not to say no. People who are the unwitting servants
to their master calendars. People whose own impulses, in
conjunction with the ninety-mile-an-hour culture swirl-
ing around them, leave them feeling they don't ever have

permission to step out of line, to hop off the merry-go-round, to decide for themselves it's time to close up shop and go home.

That's a slave talking. Hear it? "I can't just . . . not . . . can I?"

No, you can't. Not if you're a slave.

But . . . you can if you're free.

And guess what? "It was for freedom that Christ set us free; therefore keep standing firm and do not be subject again to a yoke of slavery" (Gal. 5:1). Enough *can* be enough—not just on our calendars but in every area of our lives. Then we can sit back in the freedom that helps us start again tomorrow with our spirits rested, alert, and renewed.

Wonder what kind of shock wave would reverberate through enemy headquarters if a woman decided to take her stand on that kind of battle plan? What if you found the voice to utter that dirty little word—"no"—without shouldering the least bit of guilt or shame from it? Sure, we're called to serve, and serving often requires sacrifice. Not everything we're tasked with doing should be expected to fit conveniently into our day. But a free woman possesses the God-given ability to know when He is truly asking her to do something—as well as the God-given ability to know when He's *not*. Then she has the God-given discernment to know her limits and the authority to know when she needs "to cease, to stop, to pause"—accepting the gentle yoke of

Jesus instead of the tyrannical yoke of slavery. "For My yoke is easy," He said, "and My burden is light" (Matt. 11:30).

Your Father just wants you to be you. And that means not having to be two of you to get it all done.

Jesus was the poster child for this kind of margin. Listen to Him: "The Son can do nothing of Himself, unless it is something He sees the Father doing; for whatever the Father does, these things the Son also does in like manner" (John 5:19). Even Jesus—the Son of God—realized that *everything* wasn't supposed to be *His* thing to do. He only did what He saw the Father doing. Nothing more. Nothing less.

Not every *good* thing is a *God* thing. Plain and simple. Because even good things can culminate in slavery.

Second, see how *fear* and *insecurity* come into play in your pressures. Those words always have an enemy ring to them, don't they? Satan's ploy is to make you believe your core value as a person is tied to how much work you do, how much activity you can accomplish, how much stuff you can accumulate, how much business you can generate. In order to possess any worth under this system—just like Israel under Pharaoh's rule—you've got to be able to rattle off everything you've been doing, one by one, adding it all up into a big gob of bullet points and checklists that ought to impress anybody.

But why? Who's drawing the measuring lines? And who's declaring you deficient for not meeting them? Who's setting the bar and the benchmarks of your approval? Who's saying you're worth nothing more than the overall tally of your output?

You know *exactly* who.

He's not much unlike the brutal overlords who held the power of intimidation over the Hebrew slaves in ancient Egypt. Survival was totally dependent on avoiding the cruelty of these relentless taskmasters. And the only way to do it—the only way of gaining any semblance of favor—was through working and producing. Through unending activity.

It's the same brand of heavy-handedness that's still being perpetuated against us today—the kind of internal and external pressure that turns busyness into a badge of honor. Our insecurities make us fear what others will say or think of us (or of our kids) if we don't do everything they deem to be required of us or don't acquire enough to impress them. It's why we turn Christian living into legalism, for fear that God will be displeased if we don't rigorously stick to the program. It's why we don't know how to sit still. It's why we're so rarely satisfied with where we are or what we have. It's why we can't embrace the one thing we're doing now because of the dozen other things we're *not* doing while we're over here doing *this*.

It's intimidation. It's based totally on lies and fear. Fear that we won't have enough. Fear that we won't *be* enough. Fear that we'll fail and will no longer come off looking as perfect as we want to appear. Fear that somebody else who's

working harder and moving faster will get what was supposed to be ours.

But as a dear friend and wise mentor recently said to
me, "God doesn't want something *from* you. He wants something *for* you." Your value is not in what you *do* (as if you
could ever do enough) but in who you *are* (as if you could
ever be more loved and accepted by Him than you already
are).

This, too, is what Sabbath is meant to communicate.
You don't need to keep pushing, rushing, gathering, hus-
tling. You've already received approval from the only One
whose approval really matters. He has stamped *His* value on
you, and that is enough. Even the activities He gives you to
steward are not given to see how many balls you can juggle,
but instead so you can participate with Him in staking a
kingdom claim on the patches of ground where you live.
Sure, there's sweat involved. Sore muscles. Dirt under your
pretty fingernails. But these endeavors and hobbies and
accumulated possessions of yours are meant to bring joy,
to enhance relationships, to develop your gifts, to swell you
with His blessing and contentment. They're not supposed to
be nothing but *pressure*.

So if that doesn't square with how you're feeling very
often at the end of the day, you're being bullied by a liar.
You're being motivated by fear and insecurity. You're being
intimidated by your enemy's cruel application of pressure
against you. And you don't need to put up with it any longer.

One additional thing, but a very important thing: pressure is often a mask for *idolatry*. Easy not to notice how every time Moses approached Pharaoh throughout the early part of Exodus, declaring God's words to the Egyptian ruler, he didn't just say, "Let My people go," like the lyrics to the old spiritual says. He said, "Let My people go, *so that they may worship Me*" (Exod. 9:1 HCSB, *author emphasis*). Said it about a dozen times. Look it up. There was a specific reason for their release.

The purpose of Israel's liberty from bondage—and the purpose behind your own liberty from the slavery of undue pressure—is not merely freedom for freedom's sake. God's purpose in giving you Sabbath spaces amid your full, productive life is to help you be uninhibited in your devotion, service, and worship of Yahweh. Margin keeps you from marginalizing God.

When our lives are packed to the brim with things that squeeze God to the periphery, it's a sure sign we've replaced our devotion to God with a love for something else. The pressure to perform, for example, often means you've made an idol of your reputation. The pressure to maintain a ridiculously jam-packed schedule: the idol of self-reliance. The pressure to maintain an impressive standard of living: the idol of achievement. The pressure to take on everything in which your kids show even the slightest interest: making an idol of your children. Our hearts can make idols of anything . . . yet sometimes be the last to realize it's happening.

The primary purpose of Sabbath margins—of saying no, when appropriate—is to diminish our devotion to all other suitors and crystallize our allegiance to God. The enemy wants other things and other people to replace God's preeminence in our schedule, in our mind, in our heart, in our home. He wants our loyalties lured away from our Creator and dispersed among a dozen others, without our even thinking about it.

Unmanageable, incessant pressure, then, is not just another nagging problem in your average day. It's an attack against your full devotion to God as your one and only Lord. It's a cosmic battle for your contentment, your peace, your rest, your sense of balance, health, and wholeness, your ability to worship attentively, to trust fully, to be free and satisfied in Christ, available to move at the invitation of His perfectly timed will. That's why alleviating these pressures is not merely fodder for self-help magazines and motivational speeches. It should also be a matter that's worth our serious prayer.

I think we've missed this connection for too long. We've been too tired and overwhelmed to see it. But now our eyes are open, and we can see the enemy's strategy is exposed. So let's use prayer, like a sharp pair of scissors, to help cut ourselves loose.

CALL TO PRAYER

This one life is all we've got. This one pass through the gauntlet of life's pressures and demands is our one chance to choose: Will we let them dominate and define us? Steal our hearts and devotion? Or will our service and adoration of the Father determine how we operate—determine what fills our plate?

Life will never stop being hard. I know that. And, yes, being our best and giving full effort is important in every area of our lives. But we have not been put here to be slaves to schedules that eat up every inch of margin from our families, our friendships, our worship, and our calling, nor to let others decide every day what our plans and priorities are supposed to be. We're not a "bondwoman" but a "free woman" (Gal. 4:31).

And it's time we started living (and praying) like one.

When we become strategic and focused in our prayer, God will not only begin the process of tearing us free, but He will weave new threads of peace, rest, and contentment into their place. And once we've experienced the radical difference these liberators can make, well . . . let's just see the enemy try taking them away from us again. He may get the best of us sometimes, but he'll at least know he's been in a battle.

Perhaps before collecting your Scriptures and developing a pointed prayer strategy in this area, you might want to start by doing a little personal inventory. It might help you be more tailored in your praying. Try identifying the most common pressures and expectations in your life that cause you fatigue, fragmentation, distress—occasionally even an emotion that borders on despair.

- Check your schedule for patterns where you're allowing yourself to be enslaved to things that aren't truly as critical, important, or indispensable as they seem.

- Check your motivations for why you say yes to so many things and why you feel such guilt and loss of importance for saying no.

- Check to see if the places where you most typically overload your time involve people or goals or interest areas that you've elevated to the status of idols.

- Check how much emphasis you place on the current status of your wardrobe, house, car, job, fitness, education, and any external measure that causes you to feel defensive, pressured to keep up and compare.

Ask the Lord for real discernment here because some of these determinations can be subtle and hard to spot. Remember, your enemy is involved, so he's sure to try blinding you to what's really underneath it all. A close friend or family member whose wisdom you trust might actually be helpful in this process as well if you'll promise to consider the validity of everything she says and reveals about you, even the things you don't quite agree with at first.

In some ways, committing to targeted prayer in this area might not feel as essential as some of the others we've addressed in this book. Pressure and busyness seem so pervasive and universal, with so little we can actually do about them. But, oh, yes we can. And, oh, yes we must. Rest and contentment are not stand-alone experiences. They trickle down through everything else that comprises your life. Without them a lot of other things go wrong and lose hope.

But by the Spirit's power helping you gain control of your schedule, creating spaces within which to breathe, obeying the principles of God's Sabbath, and establishing boundaries based on the truth of His all-wise Word, your destiny comes into clearer focus. Your worship blossoms into brilliant colors. And your day amazingly brightens into joy.

The enemy's going to hate this. Let's do it . . .

I am at rest in God alone;
my salvation comes from Him.
He alone is my rock and my salvation,
my stronghold; I will never be shaken.
(Ps. 62:1–2 HCSB)

∽

From the end of the earth I will cry to You,
When my heart is overwhelmed;

Lead me to the rock that is higher than I.
For You have been a shelter for me,
A strong tower from the enemy.
I will abide in Your tabernacle forever;
I will trust in the shelter of Your wings.

> (Ps. 61:2–4 NKJV)

᙮

He is not impressed by the strength of a horse;
He does not value the power of a man.
The LORD values those who fear Him,
those who put their hope in His faithful love.

> (Ps. 147:10–11 HCSB)

᙮

You are my hope;
O Lord GOD, You are my confidence from my
youth.
By You I have been sustained from my birth;
You are He who took me from my mother's womb;
My praise is continually of You. (Ps. 71:5–6)

᙮

I, the LORD, am your God,
Who brought you up from the land of Egypt;
Open your mouth wide and I will fill it. (Ps. 81:10)

❧

If you . . . call the Sabbath a delight
and the holy day of the LORD honorable;
if you honor it, not going your own ways,
or seeking your own pleasure, or talking idly;
then you shall take delight in the LORD,
and I will make you ride on the heights of the
    earth;
I will feed you with the heritage of Jacob your
    father,
for the mouth of the LORD has spoken.
    (Isa. 58:13–14 ESV)

❧

You will know the truth, and the truth will make
you free. (John 8:32)

❧

You shall remember that you were a slave in the land
of Egypt, and the LORD your God brought you out
of there by a mighty hand and by an outstretched
arm; therefore the LORD your God commanded you
to observe the sabbath day. (Deut. 5:15)

❧

. . . being content with what you have; for He Himself has said, "I will never desert you, nor will I ever forsake you." (Heb. 13:5)

&

Seek first the kingdom of God and His righteousness, and all these things will be provided for you. (Matt. 6:33 HCSB)

&

Delight yourself in the LORD;
And He will give you the desires of your heart.
   (Ps. 37:4)

Few things hold the potential to so drastically alter the landscape of your life as when you claim godly authority over the insane amount of unnecessary pressures you face. Be ready to see your eyes opened as you close them in prayer. One day soon a whole new kind of woman is going to be emerging from that prayer closet.

A free one. A rested one. A contented one.

YOUR HURTS

TURNING BITTERNESS TO FORGIVENESS

If I were your enemy, I'd use every opportunity to bring old wounds to mind, as well as the people, events, and circumstances that caused them. I'd try to ensure that your heart was hardened with anger and bitterness. Shackled through unforgiveness.

Hollow and dull. That's how my prayers felt. Like they were ricocheting off the walls of a deep, empty cave. And I wasn't sure why. I just knew I was growing really tired of it. Because once you've tasted the bold, intense flavors of fervent prayer, the blandness of living with anything less than pure freedom and intimacy with God is almost more than you can stand. You miss it. You crave it. Especially, like I said, when you've wracked your brain and can't figure out why it's suddenly, mysteriously gone.

Those were some of the spiritual doldrums I was experiencing when a friend mentioned a book on prayer written in the mid-seventies and asked if I had read it. Based on her description and recommendation, sounded like it might be just what I needed. So I immediately ordered it, and it wasn't long before God spoke to my heart through a passage of Scripture quoted in one of the early chapters of the book: "Now if anyone has caused pain," Paul wrote in 2 Corinthians, referring to a matter that had grown divisive in the Corinthian church he was addressing, "you should rather turn to forgive" (2 Cor. 2:5, 7 ESV).

Suddenly my heart burned in my chest.

But I kept reading.

"You should rather turn to forgive and comfort him, or he may be overwhelmed by excessive sorrow. So I beg you to affirm your love for him. For this is why I wrote, that I might test you and know whether you are obedient in everything . . . so that we would not be outwitted by Satan; for we are not ignorant of his designs." (vv. 7–9, 11 ESV)

Forgive *and* comfort.

Obedience in everything.

Outwitted by Satan.

Ignorant of his designs.

This simple passage struck me. Hit me with a deep, inner conviction that only God's Spirit can give. I realized in that moment what I'm about to share with you now in this chapter, a truth that reinvigorated my prayer life and set me back on track. It's this: Unforgiveness is a strategic "design," craftily implemented by your enemy to "outwit" you, to cripple your effectiveness in prayer and your power to stand against him victoriously. Which is why, if I were your enemy, I would do everything possible to keep you from forgiving anyone and everyone who's done you any wrong.

Such was the case with me. And these verses had brought all the specifics roaring back to my attention.

The offender in question (and there was no question in my mind who it was) hadn't done anything particularly brutal to me, nothing that would alter the whole trajectory of my life or anything. But it was enough to drive a wedge between the two of us and dig a tender spot in my heart.

After years of work and prayer and patience and sacrifice, a few exciting things were beginning to materialize in my personal life and ministry, the kinds of things that make you smile right before you fall asleep at night and then again first thing in the morning. I'd shared some of these happenings with a few close friends who I thought would celebrate with me, but this one person's response had been

. . . not rude perhaps, but critical. Far less than supportive and enthusiastic. And then as days, weeks, and months went on, she'd grown rather reclusive and quiet toward me. Distant and disengaged.

I thought maybe I was being a bit overly sensitive. But a few other people had begun to notice it too, without my needing to bring it to their attention. Even *they* were unnerved by the cold shoulder she was throwing me. So I guessed it really *was* as obvious as I'd thought. Wasn't all in my head. And none of us could understand exactly what her problem was.

I actually thought I was handling it the best way I knew how—mostly by trying my best to be where she *wasn't,* as often as possible. But on those occasions when keeping a safe distance wasn't possible, that's when I could tell this whole thing was becoming a bigger deal to me than I was letting on. A lot of emotion would bubble to the surface when she was around. I was stewing. The feelings inside when I thought of her or saw her weren't doing me any good. And even though I tried to push them out of mind, fairly justified that I'd done nothing wrong to cause this kind of reaction from someone . . . still, the blockage kept showing up with this person's name on it. And wouldn't go away.

Then came 2 Corinthians 2:5–7.

Forgive.

Comfort.

Obedience.

Outwitted.

Designs.

God and I—we went round and round while I debated with Him (and *without* Him) the necessity of this bit of conviction. Because maybe, *maybe,* if forgiveness had been the only thing on the table, I might have been willing to oblige a bit easier. I did, in fact, at His insistence, forgive her. In my mind at least. Set her free from the debt I thought she owed me for making me feel so awful, so uneasy, for so long. I thought the Lord, seeing my sincerity in drawing up an internal declaration of forgiveness toward her, might cut me some slack and just forget the other part. You know, that part about offering comfort . . . to *her?*

But under the circumstances, under the specifics of His conviction, I knew He wanted more. He wanted me to show comfort to this one who had offended me. This was the only way I could be "obedient in *everything*" . . . in *this* thing. And I knew it. No, my flesh didn't want to give this person the time of day, much less the dignity of a response. But my resistance to what God's Word and command were saying clued me in beyond any doubt that I'd allowed a root of bitterness to spring up within my heart. And it was choking out some stuff I missed and that really mattered to me. And *this* was the part that was by demonic design.

So finally, one sunny day, I took my forgiveness over to her house in the form of a little meal I'd prepared. We talked. We ate together. And touched by a measure of kindness from me that could only come from the Holy Spirit (I promise you), she melted into tears in my presence.

You know what I found out that day? This will surprise you, I think. It surprised me. Even while I'd been the one growing hurt and angry by her attitude, by the minute, she'd been quietly struggling within her own heart over all of this discord too. She told me how she'd been wrestling with insecurities and other issues, enough that she was actually losing sleep and appetite. Plus, the sense of isolation she'd been increasingly feeling when others, who'd been a tad cold toward her in response to her treatment of me, had become a heavy burden on her shoulders. I began to realize what Paul meant in that passage from 2 Corinthians 2 when he said that "excessive sorrow" can overwhelm. But now, through forgiveness and a simple act of kindness, the ice was breaking, along with the enemy's design—not only his design to ruin a friendship but also to ruin my prayer life in the process.

The next time I hit my knees, the echo of that long, lonely cavern gave way to the floodgates of God's grace, pouring out over me in a fresh, fantastic way.

No longer "outwitted" by the devil.

Forgiveness instead.

Because forgiveness matters.

I know this personal example I've shared is a light one, especially when compared to the deeply wounding, life-altering offense or abuse you may have suffered. (Trust me,

I could've called up other, more difficult illustrations from my own life too.) But even this low-level infraction makes a point and speaks to a purpose that applies to every offense that comes against us. Your enemy wants you long-term angry. And he can use even the lightest offense to do it. He wants you to be a bitter woman behind that beautiful face. He wants your heart coated with the calluses of resentment, crippled by offenses from your past. Unforgiveness is his design to "outwit" you—to keep you not only bruised and bleeding but unable to experience any power in your prayers or intimacy with your Father.

Nobody needs to tell you how bad you're hurting from the injustices in your life. Even people who've suffered similar abuses or offenses as yours could never completely understand how your own rejections feel. Yours are personal and private and seemingly impossible to forgive.

But forgive anyway. Not because it's easy but because your enemy gets exactly what he wants from you otherwise. *Forgive anyway.* Not lightly and quickly but ferociously and fervently. Not only for the other person but mostly for *you*— so you can be free and full and whole and complete.

Sit down here with me for a minute where we can almost clasp each other's hands across the table, and listen to me closely: If you feel utterly, hopelessly, intolerably resistant toward forgiving this person or these people who've offended you, don't consider yourself a random victim. *The devil is behind this.* He has ridden the coattails of your anger right into the depths of your soul where he has carefully calculated your demise. He's been strategizing how to suck all the power out of your prayer life. Out of your *whole* life. He's likely the same one who started the whole mess to begin with. The same one who stirred up enough sin in another person to tempt them into doing whatever they did to you, into saying whatever they said to you, into feeling however they felt about you—perhaps how they *still* feel about you, even now. Or even if he didn't start it, he's the same enemy who jumped onto the bandwagon of a bad situation in your life, hoping to make sure it didn't merely affect your finances or your job or the status of a friendship but instead pierced deeply into your heart. Where he could keep twisting it. Inflaming it. Where almost any memory or passing thought of it could poke at you, pick at you, draw blood, inflict new damage.

Make no mistake, it is *his* doing. By specific design. Hurting you once wasn't enough. Those times when the original incidents happened, times when you were mistreated or betrayed or belittled—nooo, that level of pain just *wasn't quite enough* for him. He wanted more. He wanted permanent loss. Personality change. He wanted to redefine how you thought about God, about yourself, about others, even about those people who truly love you and intend only good for you. He wanted you fixated and patterned in your thinking so that few things would seem more dear or desirable to you than paying them back, getting your revenge. He wants you sobbing . . . or better yet, just seething, the kind of emotion that doesn't come out in crying and visible reactions but instead just cooks inside of you where the heat has no place to escape, where the tears pool up and stagnate, creating a petri dish of toxic emotions that you're forced to keep breathing. He wants you baking in unforgiveness until your spiritual life is hard and crisp around the edges. Lifeless. Comatose.

But Jesus . . . He wants you free. That's what He created you for.

"Forgive us our debts," He taught us to pray, "as we also have forgiven our debtors" (Matt. 6:12), followed a couple of verses later by this corollary statement: "For if you forgive others for their transgressions, your heavenly Father will also forgive you" (v. 14).

Might want to go back and read those verses again carefully, despite how familiar they may be to you. These words of Jesus suggest a connection between the way we handle others' offenses against us and the way God handles our offenses against Him.

Now the whole counsel of Scripture affirms that our salvation (our eternal security with God) is based solely on the work of Jesus on the cross. No action or inaction on our part (such as struggling to forgive someone who's wounded you) can sever the covenant of grace He's made with us. But *something* at least happens to our experience with the Father when we persist in holding others' sins against them.

Unforgiveness puts us in prime position for demonic influence and activity to take advantage of us. (See the parable of the unforgiving servant in Matthew 18:21–35 for one descriptive example.) And anything that dampens or deadens the freedom that God's mercy is meant to give us—can it really be worth holding onto?

Listen, God knows how to deal with sin. Our sin, their sin. When you choose to forgive someone, you're not wiping their actions away as if the bad things didn't happen, giving people a free pass from the harm they've caused. You're just sparing yourself the burden of working two extra jobs—being judge and jury for how justice is meted out in this situation. Why not let someone relieve you of the pressure—Someone who actually knows what He's doing? And Someone who's just waiting right now to talk with you about it?

His forgiveness, my friend . . . is freedom.

Yes, *His* forgiveness. *His* forgiveness of *you* is what makes *your* forgiveness possible toward *others*. Realize you are lying back already in a vast blue ocean of forgiveness—same as me, same as all of us who've been redeemed through the blood of Jesus. So there's more than enough of His forgiveness splashing around you to extinguish all the flames of rage, hatred, bitterness, or animosity your enemy may have ignited within you. Remembering what Christ's redemption has done for you will make you eager to do it for another.

"You were dead in your trespasses and sins . . . but God, being rich in mercy, because of His great love with which He loved us . . . made us alive together with Christ" (Eph. 2:1, 4–5). Start from that point, and then you can much more determinedly give mercy to others because it's so lavishly given to you.

Genuine freedom and renewed fervency are waiting for you on the other side of forgiveness. And the forgiveness you don't have any desire to give right now can be amazingly enabled through prayer. When galvanized with the living truth of God's Word, fervent prayer is the bucket that can dip down into the reserves of God's strength and pull up all the resolve you need for releasing other people from what they owe you. He can produce the healing we so desperately need, before we continue down these same old broken roads that only end up hurting other people—children, grandchildren, people who had nothing to do with this matter at all, except to be within proximity of our resentful responses.

Prayer gets at the truth. The truth of what happened? Yes. If that's really what took place, then yes. The real facts and details don't change as you get real with God in prayer. But get ready for some other pieces of information to bubble up to the surface as well, as the Spirit and the Scripture come together in agreement on how you need to handle things. The enemy, of course, will want you to balk at this part. He's been banking on keeping these solutions hidden from you and convincing you that anger and bitterness are the most productive, protective ways of managing the situation. And yet honest prayer, conducted with an open heart and an open copy of God's Word, will be sure to present you with truth.

Like the truth I got that day from 2 Corinthians.

Forgive.

And comfort.

Is the Lord possibly asking you to comfort your offender as well? Maybe. Maybe not. There's not one answer for this. I'm certainly not saying that a gesture of goodwill is always necessary or even possible. And the truth is, we're never guaranteed a positive response when we do. Yet your willingness—your *obedience*, if it's what the Lord is asking you to do—to go, to express kindness, to smile, to nod, to be generous and show concern—is a tremendous test of godly surrender and humility. It's a way of finding out if the forgiveness you claim to feel toward someone contains roots that run deeper than the roots of resentment did.

Best of all, it brands you as a woman who is in no way going to be "outwitted by Satan" or "ignorant of his designs."

If we want to be women of serious, fervent prayer, the Scripture will always lead us here. To forgiveness. In some form. In some fashion. Forgiveness is God's command. And it also comes with a promise that He will provide us the companion power to pull it off. Don't expect any other solution to work or to change anything, except for the worse.

And don't expect to experience freedom, peace, or rest from your anger until you do.

CALL TO PRAYER

God's Word is what you and I are going to be taking into our prayer strategy—a strategy that, yes, possibly holds the potential of benefitting your offender. And yet it *absolutely ensures* a benefit for you.

Freedom.

"It was for freedom that Christ set us free" (Gal. 5:1). I've quoted this verse before in the book, but it's worth repeating often, in all kinds of contexts. So why don't you underline it this time so I won't need to say it again. This verse has followed me around through life from my teenage and college years till now, and it has formed sort of an immovable object that Satan is forever forced to work around to get to my heart. Here, just one more time for good measure . . . "It was for freedom that Christ set us free," the Bible says. For *freedom.* He wants us *free.*

Think back to everything you know about Jesus and the many demonstrations of His love toward the hurting and mistreated—to the point of being mistreated Himself, again and again, up to and including His brutal torture and murder. Why? Because "the Spirit of the Lord is upon Me," He said . . . "to proclaim release to the captives, and recovery of sight to the blind, to set free those who are oppressed" (Luke 4:18).

To set us free.

To fan fresh air into the stagnant rooms of your heart. To sweeten the taste in your mouth where bitterness and unforgiveness have soured your appetite for spiritual things.

To set . . . you . . . free.

There's nothing bad in your life the devil won't try to make worse. But "the merciful man does himself good" (Prov. 11:17). The merciful woman too. So upon these truths, craft a prayer strategy of freedom and forgiveness . . .

Whenever you stand praying, forgive, if you have anything against anyone, so that your Father who is in heaven will also forgive you your transgressions. (Mark 11:25)

∽

Let all bitterness and wrath and anger and clamor and slander be put away from you, along with all malice. Be kind to one another, tender-hearted, forgiving each other, just as God in Christ also has forgiven you. (Eph. 4:31–32)

∽

Never take your own revenge, beloved, but leave room for the wrath of God, for it is written,

"Vengeance is Mine, I will repay," says the Lord. "But if your enemy is hungry, feed him, and if he is thirsty, give him a drink; for in so doing you will heap burning coals on his head." Do not be overcome by evil, but overcome evil with good. (Rom. 12:19–21)

⎯⎯

Do not let the sun go down on your anger, and do not give the devil an opportunity. (Eph. 4:26–27)

⎯⎯

Strive for peace with everyone, and for the holiness without which no one will see the Lord. See to it that no one fails to obtain the grace of God; that no "root of bitterness" springs up and causes trouble, and by it many become defiled. (Heb. 12:14–15 ESV)

⎯⎯

Love your enemies and pray for those who persecute you, so that you may be sons of your Father who is in heaven. (Matt. 5:44–45)

⎯⎯

As those who have been chosen of God, holy and beloved, put on a heart of compassion, kindness, humility, gentleness and patience; bearing with one another, and forgiving each other, whoever has a complaint against anyone; just as the Lord forgave you, so also should you. (Col. 3:12–13)

〜

If he sins against you seven times a day, and returns to you seven times, saying, "I repent," forgive him. (Luke 17:4)

〜

. . . because your sins have been forgiven through Jesus. (1 John 2:12 NLT)

The Father's shoulders are broad enough for you to cry on, strong enough to absorb with compassion whatever you need to vent to Him from the depths of your broken heart. But they are also able to lift you from the quicksand of old hurts and wounds, setting your "feet upon a rock" and putting "a new song" on your lips (Ps. 40:2–3), a song of . . .

- *Praise:* Thank Him for championing your freedom, even at the cost of your comfort.
- *Repentance:* Ask the Lord to forgive you for harboring unforgiveness in your heart. Confess any hatred, any bitterness, any harmful actions made in

anger toward others. As you sense God's forgiveness toward you for your sin, extend it to them for theirs.

- *Asking:* Record the name of the person or persons who've hurt you. And then speak their names out loud while asking for a heart that can genuinely forgive and release them from the debt you feel they owe.

- *Yes:* Commit to responding actively in any way God's Spirit might urge you to do so.

I sense courage coming from your prayer closet.

And the sweet smell of forgiveness . . . and freedom.

YOUR RELATIONSHIPS

UNITING IN A COMMON CAUSE

$\backsim$

If I were your enemy, *I'd work to create division between you and other Christians, between groups of Christians, anyone with the potential for uniting in battle against me and my plans. I'd keep you operating individually, not seeing your need for the church or tying yourself too closely to its mission. Strength in numbers and unity of purpose . . . I would not allow things like these to go unchecked.*

Friendly fire is the term used in military circles to describe soldiers killed in the line of duty by their own fellow fighters. Various military reports put the estimate of wartime deaths and other incidents attributable to friendly fire as high as 20 percent, some even higher. Imagine the added sense of devastation that staggers a young wife or a set of parents when that uniformed chaplain comes to the door to deliver the news of their loved one's death. Killed in defense of their country, yes, but . . . killed by one of their own? The senselessness. The pointlessness. The pain of loss, deepened even further by the pain of *needless* loss.

Sadly, this type of tragedy isn't only a reality on foreign battlefields; it's also happening far too frequently on ours. The number of wounded on the military record books pales in comparison to the number of human hearts that have been disparaged and broken by fellow believers, by people who were *supposed* to be fighting *with* us, not *against* us— like the person we exchanged rings with, or the lifelong friend we shared our secrets with, or the fellow congregants we go to church with.

But when it happens in these circles, it's no accident. Friendly fire in the church or in our most vital relationships is almost always code for enemy activity. He knows his odds of success jump markedly whenever he can cause heart-wrenching division between us, isolate one or two of us, and separate us into warring or stonewalled camps. We cannot leave these kinds of openings for the enemy to infiltrate.

So one of our most important strategies—a call for our most fervent praying—must be to stand against all forms of disharmony in our relationships and to battle for oneness among ourselves and all of God's people. We owe it to the Lord and we owe it to one another. The gospel we share in common is meant to continue to be shared together, both the giving and receiving of grace, inspiring each of us to pure living and spiritual fervency so the gospel can shine outward to others through our loving, enriching relationships.

Together, we are a mighty force. Satan knows that.

And by remaining united, we let him *feel* that.

The grand purposes of Christian living travel far beyond our own personal battles and border wars. The enemy knows full well that our one little candle, even if carefully, consistently trimmed and manicured—even if we're sure we're right and other people are wrong—can only produce so much heat and can only cause him so much mischief. But when we expand our prayer closets to include prayers for our circle of relationships and the shared community in our churches, suddenly we've unharnessed a live wire within his control center, shooting off sparks, fishtailing along the floor, causing alarms to blare throughout his headquarters.

He hates—*hates!*—when God's people get their act together, when we're unified as a couple, a family, a local church, as well as the global, "capital-C" Church. He hates when we're all praying for one another's needs and potential and mission and unity, going to the throne for (and even with) those around us and closest to us.

The hallmark, the true pearl of God's work on earth that frustrates the enemy's plans to no end, is this mysterious gelling of people from various backgrounds, experiences, personality types, races, and traditions—the kinds of differences that should easily keep us from being able to get along, much less to work together for kingdom purposes or to care how one another is growing in faith and perseverance. They're the kinds of things that make the option of friendly fire seem unavoidable, perhaps even appealing on occasion.

The Bible calls these natural obstacles between us a "dividing wall" (Eph. 2:14). But the power of the gospel changes all of that, breaking down the wall and bridging all potential sources of division that conspire to keep us apart and fighting. Our job now is to make sure we're clinging to that gospel and not letting personal, friendly-fire skirmishes hammer away at our unity from the inside.

If we're not praying for oneness—seriously, specifically, strategically—we're leaving our hopes for togetherness to the fickle weather patterns of emotion, misunderstanding, and imposed pressure from outside sources and circumstances. We're giving the enemy room and access to scout for breaks in the line, then to nudge his way into cracks in our relationships, separating us from the people we need most for maintaining our health and balance and authenticity, as well as from the shared energy and ideas required for our relationships to thrive.

Prayer is what greases the friction between us, lubricating around the grit and flecks of irritability that work themselves into the system, preventing the normal wear and tear of life from causing us to grate against or rub on one another. Instead we maintain our fluid motions, our synchronized interconnections. Prayer helps us stay focused on bigger things, on much more eternal things than the petty stuff that threatens to puff itself up beyond actual size and become some huge deal it doesn't deserve to be. In prayer we experience the kind of hard-fought *peace* that unites us into an army of soldiers for Christ.

Peace. Let's hang here for a second while we unpack the importance of that word in our spiritual vocabulary. *Peace.* The enemy is flat-out against it. And he works overtime to dismantle anything resembling it. But what's he so afraid that it might cause or lead us to do?

Let's start here: "Having been justified by faith," the Bible tells us, "we have peace with God through our Lord Jesus Christ" (Rom. 5:1). Peace *with* God. No more fear of condemnation. Unhindered access back and forth between Him and ourselves. So whatever lack of peace you or I might feel with God, and whenever we might feel it, it's always coming from a source that is *not* God because He has already blown down every door that keeps us from experiencing total peace with Him.

Strike one. The enemy doesn't like that.

To ruffle his feathers even more, our peace *with* God infuses us with the peace *of* God. It's a gift that keeps us stable and strong even when our circumstances are the

furthest thing away from being peaceful (John 14:27; 16:33).
It also acts as a guide that helps us discern God's leading
and direction toward our destiny (Col. 3:15). The peace of
God is what helps us navigate the will of God.

Strike two. *Another* thing the enemy doesn't like.

This is now officially getting worse for him. Getting bigger. Growing new body parts and appendages. On the verge
of getting out of hand, out of control.

Here, then, is why he digs in so hard in trying to separate friends and churches. It's all a desperate attempt to
avoid strike three. You see, peace *with* God is individual.
Personal. The peace *of* God—same thing. It's about *you*,
no one else. But peace with others? Now we've got wit-
nesses. Now we're moving in a pack. We've got the strength
of numbers. And that makes us more of a problem to him
than ever.

The magnet that draws other people out of darkness
toward the light and hope of Jesus Christ is so often not the
A-B-C evangelism presentation they *hear* but the one they
see—the recognizable change and difference in people who
claim to be at peace with God themselves. Friends who
forgive, sisters in Christ whose relationship is an inspira-
tion, husbands and wives who clearly love each other with a
passionate sense of loyalty and unity, churches and denomi-
nations that are known for celebrating their commonalities
more than arguing about their differences—those are the
kind of people who best entice others out of their loneliness,

pain, and despair to seek their own peace with God through Christ.

So we should not be surprised when Satan thwarts our unity as believers, in all kinds of different pairings and places where we interact with fellow Christians.

He'll do it in your *local church*. He'll stir up a faction who thinks the pastor is woefully deficient in his preaching or his time management or his leadership style or his bed-side manner. He'll create a stir over how loud they play the music in worship or how often someone's wife or daughter is allowed to sing solos. He'll divide old and young, traditional-ists versus progressives, private school kids from the public schoolers. Instead of people being able to freely exercise and emphasize their various spiritual gifts for the good of the body, he'll cause folks to see one person's ministry as being a direct competitor of another's. Division, disharmony, friendly fire. They're breaks in the line of our peace.

He'll do it in the *global church* too. He'll augment the clashes of race and economics and doctrinal stances con-cerning issues of relatively minor importance, turning them into trench warfare among fellow believers in the body of Christ, further quieting the voice of the gospel behind loud debates over our firmly held positions.

And he'll do it in your own *personal relationships* as well. Mark the ones that form the inner circle around your heart, the tribe you go into battle with, the people who are most influential in helping you stay spiritually on task and on target—people who most likely depend on you in the same way. Think of your spouse, your closest girlfriends, your accountability partners, the other participants in your discipleship group. Do you ever sense any tearing or break-down between the close bonds you share with these people? Do you occasionally grow tired of the level of commitments you've made with some of them, considering it more of an intrusion than a mutual blessing? Do you sometimes wish they wouldn't call or want anything of you tonight or wouldn't ask about how you've been managing yourself lately? Do you find yourself almost physically drawn toward gossiping and listening to stories about them or others that are less than flattering—things you'd never want them to know that you said or found so pleasurably, provocatively interesting?

I realize how easy some of these habits and attitudes can be to fall into. But each time you detect them taking shape, both in yourself as well as in others, realize you're being taunted by an opposing batter. He's pulling out every trick in his strategy book. He's working to keep you from winding up and throwing a fastball of peace right over the heart of the plate, where all he can do is stand there and watch it sail past him. He wants to keep your aim wide of the target, low and outside, hoping to get to first base and keep himself in the game. Hoping to give himself a fighting chance for as long as possible.

Because if it weren't for him trying to get in there and cause trouble, would any of us be feeling the need to nurse hurt feelings, harbor unforgiveness, belabor the gossip, or (for goodness sake) find a whole new set of friends?

He's the reason our team doesn't always want to play like one.

And I say we throw him that third strike.

And get him out of there.

CALL TO PRAYER

As you begin to develop your personalized approach to this tenth strategy, start by identifying the most common tools of division and disunity the enemy employs to destroy your key relationships. James 3:14–16 is as good a place to start as any, because this New Testament letter doesn't pull any punches . . . just says it out there the way it really is.

> If you have bitter jealousy and selfish ambition in your heart, do not be arrogant and so lie against the truth. This wisdom is not that which comes down from above, but is earthly, natural, demonic. For where jealousy and selfish ambition exist, there is disorder and every evil thing. (James 3:14–16)

Jealousy—the idea of never wanting to take a backseat to someone else's success or growth pattern. *Bitterness*—irritations that have simmered inside you long enough until they've turned into intolerable dislikes. *Selfish ambition*—the desire to dominate or come out looking better than someone else, even someone you care about. *Arrogance*—thinking you're most likely the one who's the most right whenever there's any difference of opinion. Those are just a few of the high spots from a thirty-thousand-foot sampling. There are plenty of others on the way down. But James's interpretation of the root causes behind this rotten fruit sounds fairly comprehensive. The reason they result in "disorder and every evil thing" is because they don't bear any of the earmarks of those qualities that come down to us from God, from above, but instead are "earthly, natural, *demonic.*"

Straight from the devil's domain.

So if we can pull back for a moment from whatever's creating distance and disrespect among the people we know and among the church where we worship, you can bet your bottom dollar there's a demonic tint to most of it. He's got a lot of chips invested in chipping away at our unity. And while he can't turn us into little devils ourselves, he can lure us into doing things that bear a striking resemblance. Our job as people who've caught on to his schemes is to keep the truth plastered in large letters where we can't help but see it and to pray we'll be able to sniff out his activity both in ourselves and in others . . . because we know it's doing nothing more than inserting holes in the line of our peace and unity, slowing our steady march forward. Together.

So starting today, we craft a prayer strategy with peace *in* mind, leading to peace *of* mind for ourselves and the ones we love.

Let the peace of Christ rule in your hearts, to which indeed you were called in one body. (Col. 3:15)

∽

Pursue the things which make for peace and the building up of one another. (Rom. 14:19)

∽

We are no longer to be children, tossed here and there by waves and carried about by every wind of doctrine, by the trickery of men, by craftiness in deceitful scheming. (Eph. 4:14)

∽

Let us not love with word or with tongue, but in deed and truth. (1 John 3:18)

∽

Let us not judge one another anymore, but rather determine this—not to put an obstacle or a stumbling block in a brother's way. (Rom. 14:13)

❧

Let us not become boastful, challenging one another, envying one another. (Gal. 5:26)

❧

Let us consider how to stimulate one another to love and good deeds, not forsaking our own assembling together, as is the habit of some, but encouraging one another; and all the more as you see the day drawing near. (Heb. 10:24–25)

❧

Behold, how good and how pleasant it is
For brothers to dwell together in unity!
It is like the precious oil upon the head,
Coming down the beard,
Even Aaron's beard,
Coming down upon the edge of his robes.
It is like the dew of Hermon
Coming down upon the mountains of Zion;
For there the LORD commanded the blessing—life
     forever. (Ps. 133:1–3)

❧

Make my joy complete by being of the same mind, maintaining the same love, united in spirit, intent on one purpose. Do nothing from selfishness or empty conceit, but with humility of mind regard one another as more important than yourselves; do not merely look out for your own personal interests, but also for the interests of others. (Phil. 2:2–4)

～

... so that there may be no division in the body, but that the members may have the same care for one another. (1 Cor. 12:25)

The peace of God, preserved by the prayers of God's people, is meant to forge us together in friendship and unite us in mission. And when it does, not only does it cause the people around us to sit up and notice, but it declares the manifold wisdom of God through the church "to the rulers and authorities in the heavens" (Eph. 3:10 HCSB). Unity among brothers and sisters puts Satan promptly in his place.

And that's something that ought to make us eager to be watchful, to be encouraging, to be merciful.

To be unified.

AMEN

Hesitantly.

That's how I walked through the door that very first time.

An acquaintance had recommended a Bible study group that met in someone's home in our local area. It wasn't affiliated with our church, wasn't even necessarily in the stream of our particular denominational vein. But I'd been expressing to some close friends a new hunger I'd been feeling for going deeper with God—for experiencing Him more fully. More tangibly. Wasn't sure what all of that meant exactly, just feeling slightly stuck and restless in my spiritual journey. They'd assured me that these people and this environment were exactly what I needed. I wondered, however, walking into this house for the first time, if I might have gotten myself into a bit more of a tangible experience than I'd bargained for.

These people were, well . . . different. At least different from most of the people I was accustomed to sitting around doing Bible study with. But the difference was unusual in a beautiful way. I couldn't exactly put my finger on what gave me this first impression, what made them so intriguing to me. Neither could I be sure I'd made the right decision to show up here at a stranger's house. I mean, these people didn't know *me*; I didn't know *them*. But somehow I felt comfortable. And since I was there already, I figured the only right choice was to stay and see . . . see what made this gathering so unique.

I slipped into a seat on the side. Out of the way. A few people smiled politely. Nodded. I took in my surroundings for a minute or two, and then the meeting started.

Sort of.

Because nothing really happened. Nothing official, that is. No one standing front and center. No welcome. No announcements. No opening Bible reading. Just . . .

A holy hush. Soft worship music lightly pulsed in the background, while a thick silence fell across everyone present. Some of them slipped to their knees, eyes closed, hands either folded or lifted slightly above their upturned faces. Others just sat in their chairs or on the sofas, while a few actually found spaces throughout the room where they could lie prostrate on the floor. For a solid hour these people did nothing but pray—passionate, personal prayer like I'd rarely experienced in my life. No one looked bored or hurried, as if wanting to move on to something else, to something more important or structured.

Because this—this praying—is what they'd come for.

And as I soon discovered, once I became acclimated to what was going on, this praying was what I'd unknowingly come for as well. After about twenty minutes of sitting there, surrounded by this deep crescendo of worship—totally peaceful and yet totally electric, all at the same time—tears began trailing down my face. Waves of new freedom and confident faith surged through my spirit at the power of God's presence. I then understood what accounted for the beautiful difference I'd detected when I first entered the room.

These people were committed—fervently—to prayer.

The reason I share this story—two reasons, really. The first is how contagious a commitment to serious prayer becomes when you see it. You feed off of it. You want it. As I imagine the kind of praying you've been doing while we've shared this brief journey together, as well as the prayers you'll continue to be reading and rereading from your walls and corkboards and tablets, the beauty of your praying wafts through my mind like the incense it truly is before the Lord. I love the thought of it. I love what we've shared and what we're sharing. I love knowing that a sister like you is uniting with me and with thousands of others in devoting ourselves to prayer.

But the second reason is one I couldn't have known at the time those many years ago, yet can see so clearly now as I write this final chapter and look back on that unique experience. You see, at the end of that first meeting (which, by the way, I attended faithfully for the next seven years), the person who was teaching from the Bible that day—a man I'd never met beforehand, a man who didn't know me or anything about me—looked my direction and spoke directly to me. From my vantage point he was framed between a couple of pairs of shoulders positioned between us, but he was obviously addressing *me*. ("Yes. You.") I held my breath while he told me in vivid terms that, among other things, he sensed I would have the privilege of calling many people to prayer during my lifetime. And not just to prayer but to a refreshed, renewed focus and fervency of prayer they'd never known before.

My heart burned within me as this stranger spoke what I knew to be God's very word for my life that morning. I knew then that in some way he was right. I wasn't sure how or what all of it meant. I just *knew* it would be part of my calling. My purpose. The gravity of what he said, in fact, was so profound and confirming and laced with pinpointed Scriptures and clarity that I went home and wrote down every word I could remember. I still have the notes of that experience to this day.

And now, as I look back on those notes, it's all clear to me—*you* were a part of that first meeting. God had you in mind that day. He knew that years later we'd be here together in this book, our hearts stirred together for fervent prayer.

In fact, over the past decade or so, I've had the privilege of encouraging many women in their prayer lives—never dreaming I'd write a book about it someday. I started first at my home church in Dallas, and then (as God gave me opportunity) at our ministry's conferences in different parts of the country. To this day we always set aside a part of the program for the women in attendance to write out their most heartfelt requests and prayers on a card we provide. Then we ask them to bring their card during a moment of worship and lay it alongside all the others on the steps at the front of the platform. Then I lead the entire group in corporate prayer for the hundreds and hundreds of needs that are so visibly expressed before us. When the event is over, we collect all the cards. Then each woman takes the written request of another woman home with her, promising to post it in a place where she'll be reminded of it and will commit to pray for it fervently for the next seven full days. So while one woman is covering the request of another—likely a stranger she may never see again this side of eternity—another woman is praying for her.

After all these years, all these events, and all of these requests, I don't know how many thousands of women have participated in this exercise. All I know for sure is that since that meeting years ago, I've sensed something highly important happening as a result of women vocalizing their prayers on paper, narrowing down their focus onto what truly mattered most to them, and then becoming consistent and diligent in taking those prayers to the Father.

And I know without a doubt that God planned the chance for you and me to get together like this too—to unite through our passion for prayer. In fact, He whispered to me about you at that very first Bible study. I didn't know it then. But I see it clearly now.

It's you.

You're the one He had in mind.

So as we bring this book to a close, I simply want to leave you with the same words I'd share with you if I were sitting in *your* house, on *your* sofa, as we encourage each other about being devoted to our God and to prayer.

I ask you to wear this book out, girl. Make it pay for whatever you paid for it. Make prayer both your lifeline and your lifestyle. Continue to write His Word on your heart, on your hand, on those little pieces of paper I've given you, or on whatever scrap of notepad, sticky note, or stationery is your canvas of choice. Something highly important and powerful happens when you put these prayers of yours and these promises of His into words. And into action.

So stick 'em to the wall. Post them on your bathroom mirror. Adhere them to the dashboard of your car. Tape them inside your office cubicle. Put them anywhere, any-place where you're likely to see them, speak them, and have your heart transformed by them. His Word is truth, my friend. And your enemy trembles before it—because, while he'll never admit it until that great day when every knee shall bow (even his) in awed acknowledgment of God's preeminent power, he knows it's true as well. This is the beginning of the end for his influence on your life, for his arrogant assumption that he can do anything he wants with you, and you won't have the power to fight back or resist.

Oh, is he ever in for a shock.

And it all starts with those prayers.

So pray them with thanksgiving. "Be anxious for nothing," Paul said, "but in everything by prayer and supplication *with thanksgiving* let your requests be made known to God" (Phil. 4:6, author emphasis). Approach God boldly with every single need. Never with a hint of fear, guilt, or shame. But always incubate those requests in gratitude. You'll know you're trusting Him when you're simultaneously being thankful to Him . . . thankful for who He is, for what He's already done, and for what He's currently doing. If you ever don't know what to pray exactly, just start with gratitude. Affirm out loud that you know He is there and that He cares for you, no matter what difficulty may be pressing down on you at the moment. Because the fact is, He is quietly working on your behalf without any fanfare. Preparing, arranging, and planning for your good.

He is all-powerful. He is sovereign. He is right and true and eternally glorious, impervious to the enemy's intentions. And whatever comes next in your life, it will *undoubtedly* be another opportunity for you to be swept up into your Father's arms and carried through it.

And that is where you want to be. Because in His arms, you'll know the beauty of His peace—"the peace of God, which surpasses all comprehension" and which guards our hearts and minds in Christ Jesus (Phil. 4:7).

So while I know this is a battle—I know it's a daily fight—expect your fervency to lead you to a place of rest. Because God is the One who's fighting for you. And He will surely prevail.

Now unto him that is able to keep you from falling, and to present you faultless before the presence of his glory with exceeding joy, to the only wise God our Savior, be glory and majesty, dominion and power, both now and ever. Amen. (Jude 24–25 KJV)

Yes, amen.

My Notes

My Notes

My Notes

My Notes

My Notes

My Notes

PRAYER STRATEGY PAGES

A PRAYER FOR _____

_____

_____

_____

_____

_____

_____

_____

A PRAYER FOR _____

_____

_____

_____

_____

_____

_____

_____

A Prayer for _____

_____

_____

_____

_____

_____

_____

A Prayer for _____

_____

_____

_____

_____

_____

_____

A Prayer for _____

_____

_____

_____

_____

_____

_____

_____

A Prayer for _____

_____

_____

_____

_____

_____

_____

_____

A Prayer for _____

_____

_____

_____

_____

_____

_____

_____

A Prayer for _____

_____

_____

_____

_____

_____

_____

_____

A Prayer for _____

_____

_____

_____

_____

_____

_____

_____

A Prayer for _____

_____

_____

_____

_____

_____

_____

_____

A Prayer for _____

_____

_____

_____

_____

_____

_____

A Prayer for _____

_____

_____

_____

_____

_____

_____

A Prayer for _____

_____

_____

_____

_____

_____

_____

_____

A Prayer for _____

_____

_____

_____

_____

_____

_____

_____

A Prayer for _____

_____

_____

_____

_____

_____

_____

_____

A Prayer for _____

_____

_____

_____

_____

_____

_____

_____